SRA
Reading Mastery
Signature Edition

Language Arts Answer Key
Grade 2

Siegfried Engelmann
Karen Lou Seitz Davis
Jerry Silbert

Columbus, OH

SRAonline.com

Send all inquiries to this address:
SRA/McGraw-Hill
8787 Orion Place
Columbus, OH 43240-4027

ISBN: 978-0-07-612569-2
MHID: 0-07-612569-6

11 12 13 14 GPC 22 21

The **McGraw·Hill** Companies

Workbook

A (some blue)

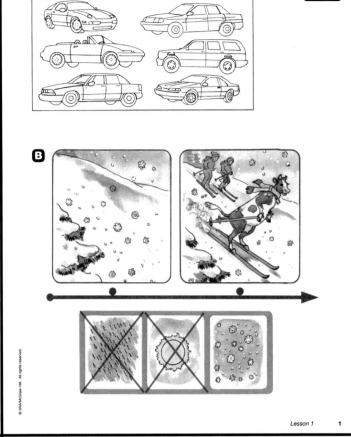

B

C

The cat was sitting in the grass.
The dog ███████████████████ .

The cat was sitting in the grass.
The dog was sitting on the chair.
(Optional: Students skip a line and write both sentences again.)

D (purple)

A

The dog was sitting on the floor.	
The cat ███████████████████.	

The dog was sitting on the floor.	
The cat was sitting on the table.	
(Optional: Students skip a line and write both sentences again.)	

B

C

D

1.

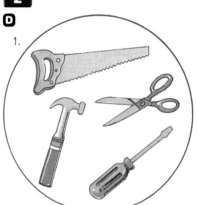

(no written answers)

2.

E

1. true (false)
2. true (false)
3. (true) false
4. true (false)
5. (true) false
6. (true) false
7. (true) false

F

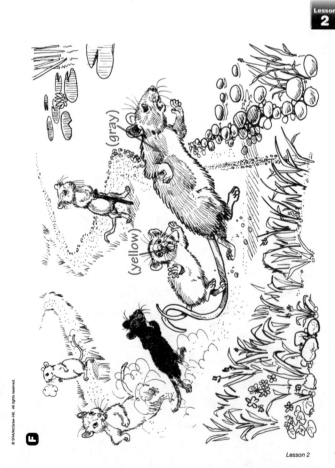

(gray)

(yellow)

2

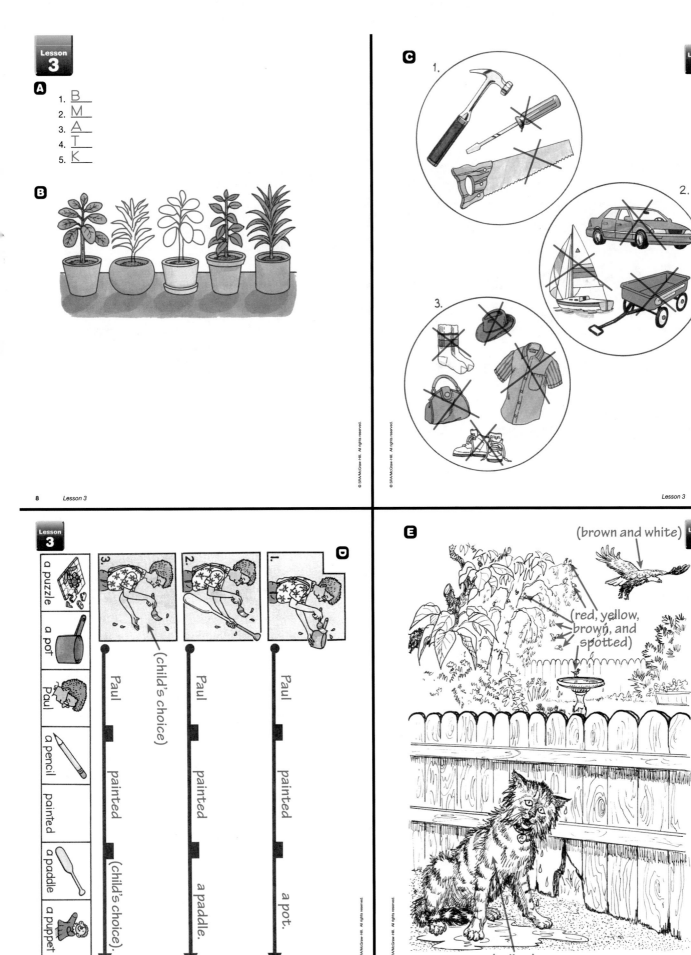

Lesson 3

A
1. B
2. M
3. A
4. T
5. K

B

8 Lesson 3

C
1.
2.
3.

Lesson 3 9

D

a puzzle

a pot

Paul

a pencil

painted

a paddle

a puppet

3. Paul painted (child's choice).

2. Paul painted a paddle.

1. Paul painted a pot.

(child's choice)

10 Lesson 3

E

(brown and white)

(red, yellow, brown, and spotted)

(yellow)

Lesson 3 11

3

A

| A boy was riding a bike. |
| A girl was riding a horse. |
| (Optional: Students skip a line and write both sentences again.) |

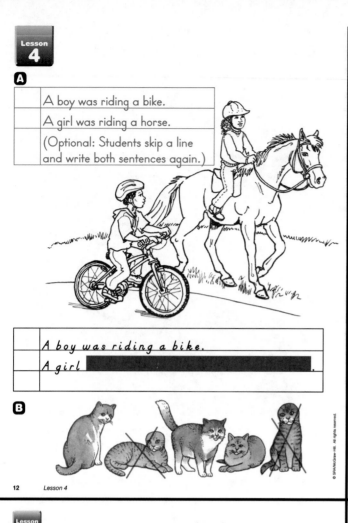

| A boy was riding a bike. |
| A girl ▮▮▮▮▮▮▮▮▮▮▮▮. |
| |

B

C

D

(blue)

(red)

(brown and white)

A

| The girl rode an elephant. |
| The boy ▮▮▮▮▮▮▮▮▮▮▮▮. |
| |

| The girl rode an elephant. |
| The boy rode a bike. |
| (Optional: Students skip a line and write both sentences again.) |

B

Some of the bugs have spots.

(spots on some bugs)

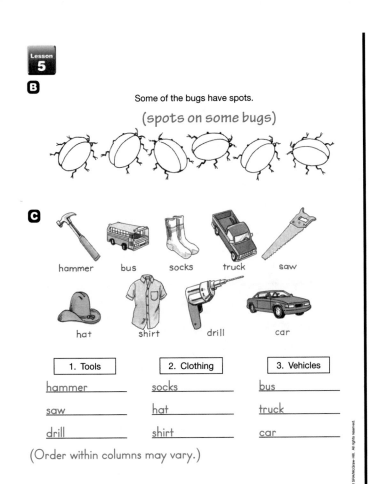

C

hammer   bus   socks   truck   saw

hat   shirt   drill   car

1. Tools	2. Clothing	3. Vehicles
hammer	socks	bus
saw	hat	truck
drill	shirt	car

(Order within columns may vary.)

(unscrunched hat)

D

A

	The boy read a paper.
	▮▮▮▮▮▮▮▮▮▮.

	The boy read a paper.
	The girl read a book.
	(Optional: Students skip a line and write both sentences again.)

B

(no written answers)

1.   2.

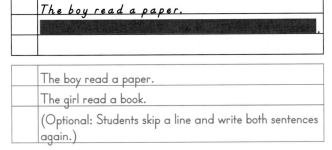

Okay, baby. _____

I will gét a stamp.

A

carrot   owl   church   banana   turtle

bear   house   hamburger   barn

1. Food	2. Buildings	3. Animals
carrot	church	owl
banana	house	turtle
hamburger	barn	bear

(Order within columns may vary.)

B

Roger	Sweetie	a hat	sat on	Clarabelle	a cake

(Child's name) ● ■ sat on ■ (child's choice).

Sweetie ● sat on a hat.

Roger ● sat on a hat.

C

1. bud   2. yus   3. fud   4. ugg
   bed   yes   fed   egg

A

The girl was standing on a chair.	
████████████████████████████████.	

The girl was standing on a chair.
The boy was standing on the floor.
(Optional: Students skip a line and write both sentences again.)

B

(no written answers)

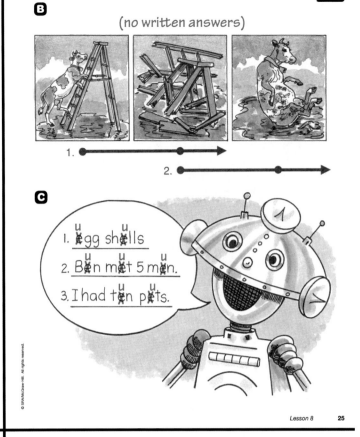

1. ●——————————●——————————→

2. ●——————————●——————————→

C

1. ĕgg shĕlls

2. Bĕn mĕt 5 mĕn.

3. I had tĕn pĕts.

D

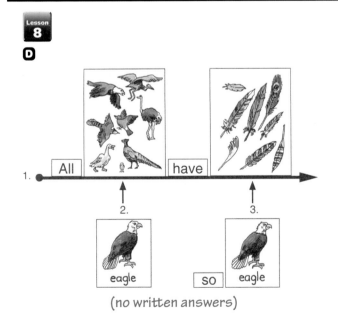

1. ●— All [birds] have [feathers] —————→

2. ↑ eagle

3. ↑ so eagle

(no written answers)

E

X = pink or purple   O = purple

7

A

A cat was sleeping on the chair.
███████████████████████████████████.

A cat was sleeping on the chair.
A dog was sleeping on the floor.
(Optional: Students skip a line and write both sentences again.)

B (no written answers)

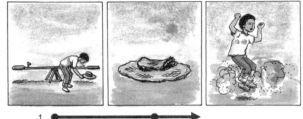

1. ●————————●————————→

2. ●————————●————————→

C

L   R

a fan   a hat   a ball   a goat   a sheep   Clarabelle

1. The third object to Bleep's right is ___Clarabelle___.

2. The first object to Bleep's left is ___a ball___.

3. The first object to Bleep's right is ___a goat___.

4. The second object to Bleep's ___(right)___ is a ___(a sheep)___.
   ___(left)___   ___(a hat)___

D

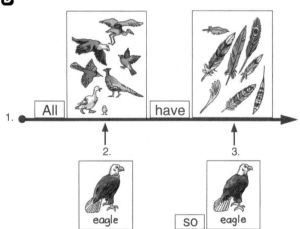

1. ●— All | 🐦 | have | 🪶 →

2. ↑ eagle

3. ↑ SO eagle

ostrich   ostrich

(no written answers)

E

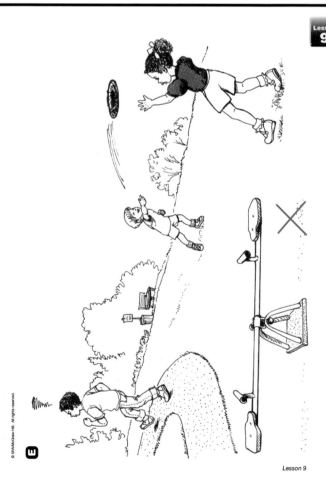

8

Test 1

Test Score [　　]

The girl was drawing a picture.
████████████████████████████.

The girl was drawing a picture.
The boy was reading a book.
(Optional: Students skip a line and write both sentences again.)

Test 1

B

a man　a sheep　a fan　　a ball　a pig　a clock

1. The third object to Clarabelle's right is ___a clock___.

2. The third object to Clarabelle's left is ___a man___.

3. The second object to Clarabelle's left is ___a sheep___.

4. The first object to Clarabelle's right is ___a ball___.

C

(spots on all bugs)

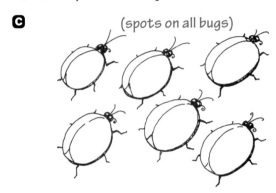

A

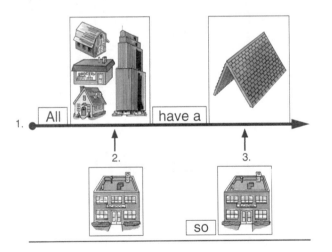

1. All [buildings] have a [roof]

2.

3.

SO

(no written answers)

---

a mouse — chased — Sweetie

a mouse — chased — Roger

(child's choice) — chased — (Child's choice)

Clarabelle	Sweetie	a skunk	chased	Roger	a mouse

9

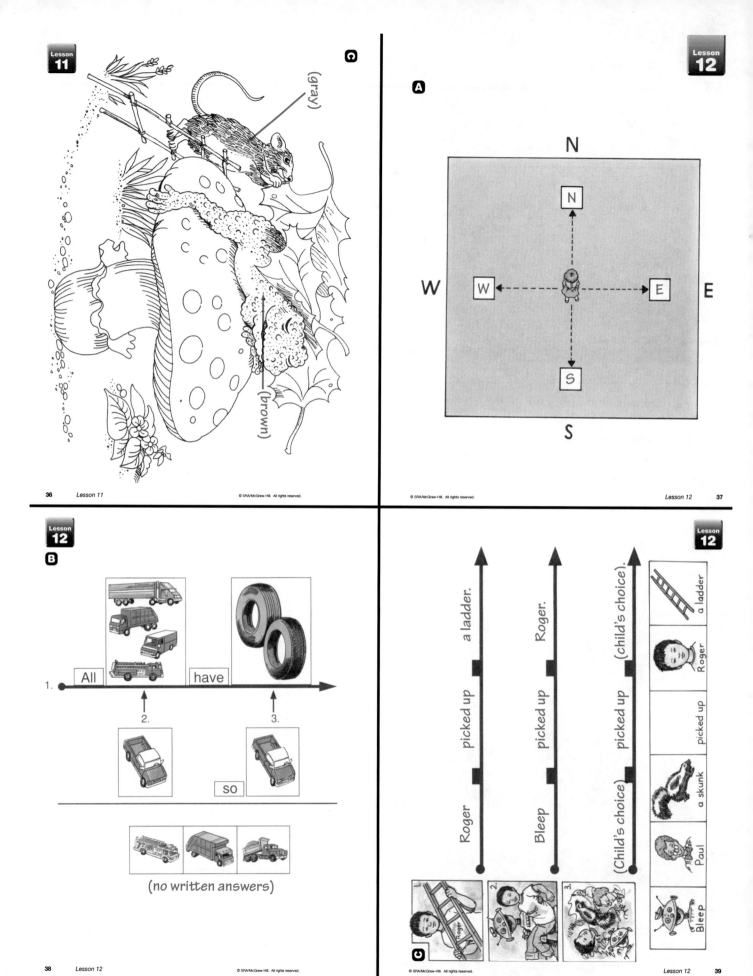

(gray)

(brown)

A

N

N

W   W ⇠ ⇢ E   E

S

S

B

1.   All   have

2.   3.

SO

(no written answers)

a ladder.   Roger.   (child's choice).

picked up   picked up   picked up

Roger   Bleep   (Child's choice)

a ladder   Roger   picked up   a skunk   Paul   Bleep

C

D

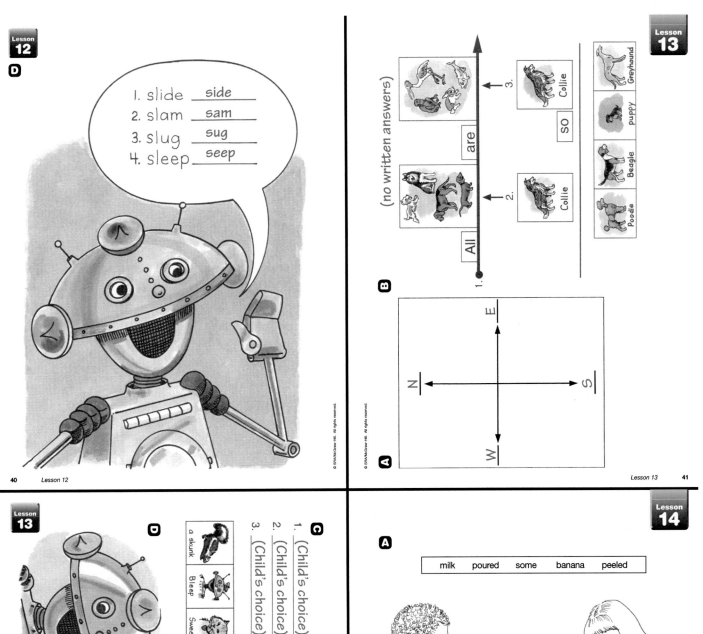

1. slide ___side___
2. slam ___sam___
3. slug ___sug___
4. sleep ___seep___

(no written answers)

B

All — are

1. 2. 3.

Collie   SO   Collie

Poodle   Beagle   puppy   Greyhound

A

N   E   W   S

C

1. (Child's choice) sat on (child's choice).
2. (Child's choice) chased (child's choice).
3. (Child's choice) picked up (child's choice).

(picture based on any sentence)

D

a skunk   Bleep   Sweetie   Roger   a hat   a toad

1. Slam the door.
2. That sled can slide.
3. A slug is sleeping.

A

milk   poured   some   banana   peeled

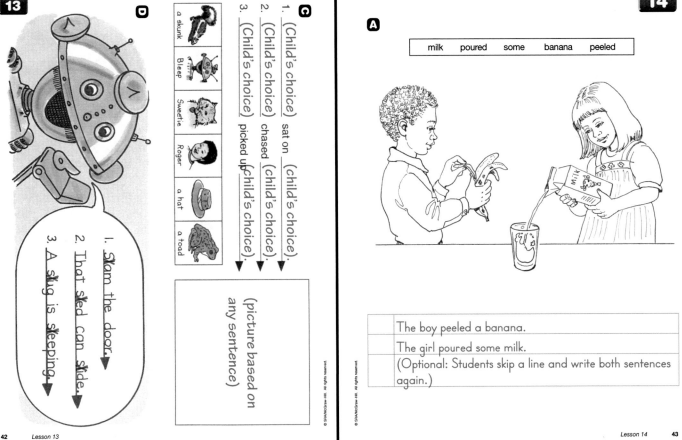

| The boy peeled a banana. |
| The girl poured some milk. |
| (Optional: Students skip a line and write both sentences again.) |

11

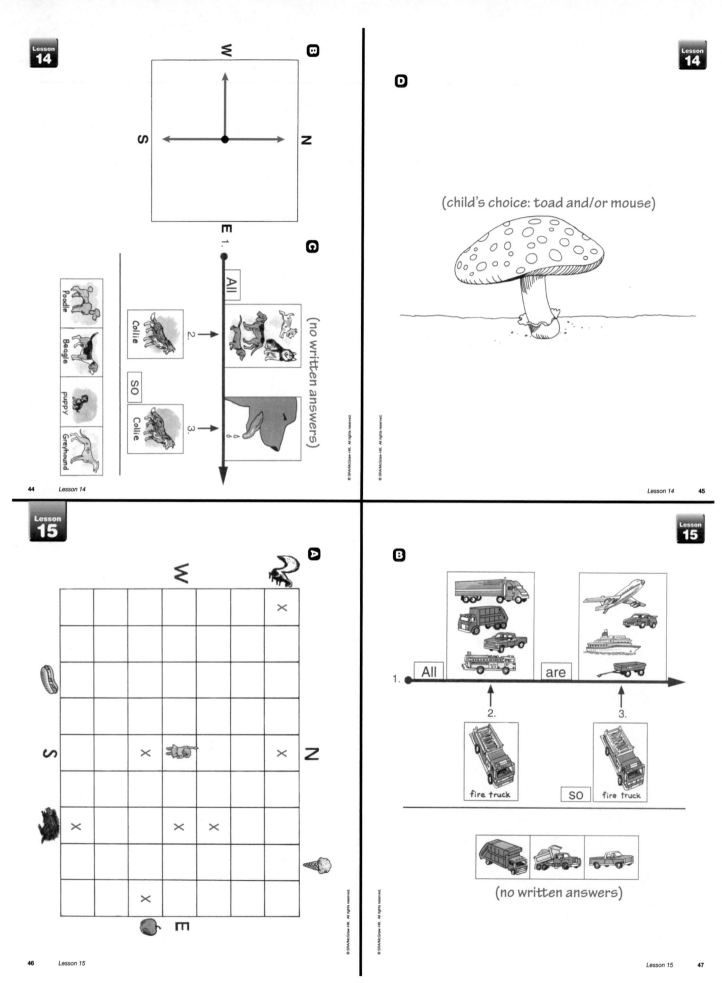

B

W

S   N

E

C

1. All

(no written answers)

2. Collie

SO   Collie

3.

Poodle | Beagle | puppy | Greyhound

D

(child's choice: toad and/or mouse)

A

W

S   N

E

B

1. All   are

2. fire truck

SO   fire truck

3.

(no written answers)

C

1. _(Child's choice)_ hugged _(child's choice)._ ►
2. _(Child's choice)_ washed _(child's choice)._ ►
3. _(Child's choice)_ talked to _(child's choice)._ ►

 a skunk Sweetie a hat Roger a clown Bleep

(picture based on any sentence)

D

A

| an apple | an orange | peeled | ate |

	Name
The girl peeled an orange.	
The boy ate an apple.	
(Optional: Students skip a line and write both sentences again.)	

B

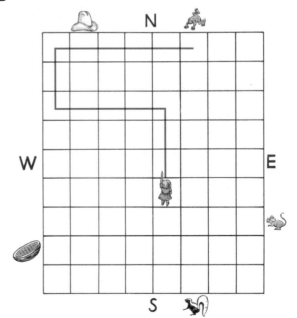

N

W E

S

13

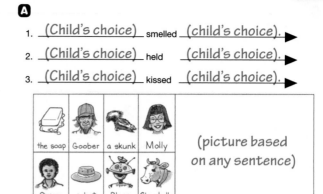

1. (Owen)
2. (Owen)   a little person
              a little person

3. (Owen)   a little person
4. Owen   a little person

A

1. ___(Child's choice)___ smelled ___(child's choice).___ ▶
2. ___(Child's choice)___ held ___(child's choice).___ ▶
3. ___(Child's choice)___ kissed ___(child's choice).___ ▶

the soap	Goober	a skunk	Molly
Owen	a hat	Bleep	Clarabelle

(picture based on any sentence)

B

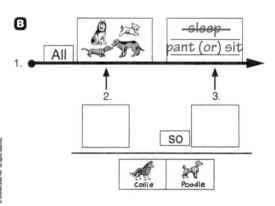

1. All   ~~sleep~~ pant (or) sit

2.   3.

SO

Collie   Poodle

C

(no written answers)

D

Dear Owen,
        Our names are Fizz and Liz
~~Hello, my name is Owen~~
                    we
and ~~I~~ live on a beautiful island.
                    big
This island is very ~~small~~.
                    big
There are many ~~small~~ animals
on this island.
            big
We have ~~tiny~~ bears and tigers
and alligators.
            big
We have ~~tiny~~ rabbits.
                        big
We also have lots of ~~tiny~~ birds.
                        big
The biggest of the ~~tiny~~ birds
is the eagle.
        no
We have bugs that are so small
you can hardly see them.

A

| standing | sitting | table | wagon |

	Name
The dog was standing in a wagon.	
The cat was sitting on a table.	
(Optional: Students skip a line and write both sentences again.)	

B

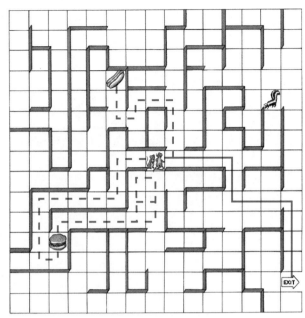

(child shows one route to hamburger)

C

(brown)

(yellow)

(red and black)

(brown)

A

| climbed | chewed | bone |

	Name
The dog chewed on a bone.	
The cat climbed a tree.	
(Optional: Students skip a line and write both sentences again.)	

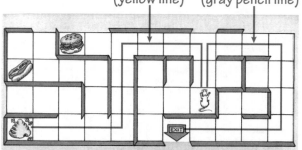

(yellow line)   (gray pencil line)

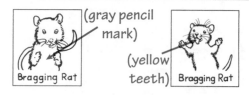

(gray pencil mark)

Bragging Rat

(yellow teeth)

Bragging Rat

Left	Right
1. Two squares to the north.	1. Two squares to the north.
2. Three squares to the east.	2. Three squares to the west.
3. Three squares to the south.	3. Three squares to the south.
4. Four squares to the west.	4. Four squares to the west.

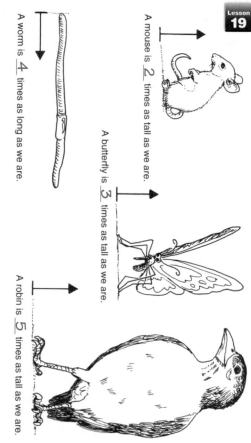

A mouse is _2_ times as tall as we are.

A butterfly is _3_ times as tall as we are.

A robin is _5_ times as tall as we are.

A worm is _4_ times as long as we are.

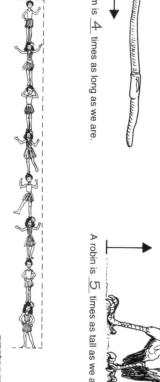

Lesson 20—Test 2

A

popcorn	reading	eating

	Name
The girl was eating popcorn.	
The boy was reading a book.	
(Optional: Students skip a line and write both sentences again.)	

Lesson 20—Test 2

Test Score

B

north
east
south
west

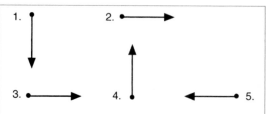

1. Arrow 1 points _south_

2. Arrow 2 points _east_

3. Arrow 3 points _east_

4. Arrow 4 points _north_

5. Arrow 5 points _west_

A

1.

Everybody found something.

Goober found (child's choice).

Liz found (child's choice).

I found (child's choice).

2.

Everybody painted something.

Roger painted (child's choice).

Molly painted (child's choice).

I painted (child's choice).

3.

Everybody ran into something.

Clarabelle ran into (child's choice).

Owen ran into (child's choice).

I ran into (child's choice).

B

(picture based on any sentence)

(picture based on any sentence)

A

next	box	chair

	A dog sat next to a chair.
	A cat sat next to a box.
	(Optional: Students skip a line and write both sentences again.)

B

(no written answers)

Hounds   **Work Dogs**

C

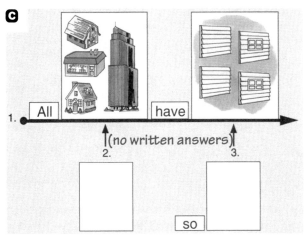

17

A

1. Basset
H

2. Collie
W

3. Beagle
H

4. German shepherd
W

5. Saint Bernard
W

6. Greyhound
H

B

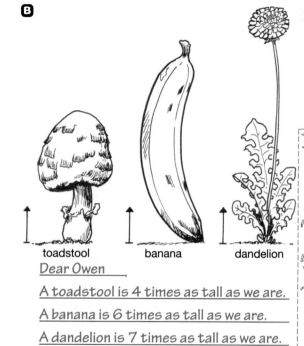

toadstool   banana   dandelion

Dear Owen,

A toadstool is 4 times as tall as we are.

A banana is 6 times as tall as we are.

A dandelion is 7 times as tall as we are.

_____

_____

_____

From Fizz and Liz

A | sawed | painted | woman | board

| The girl sawed a board. |
| The woman painted a wall. |
| (Optional: Students skip a line and write both |
| sentences again.) |

B

Not-Class

Class   (no written answers)

18

C

A

B

(brown toads
on toadstools)

Toadstools

(brown)

Where is Jenny the
toad in the afternoon?

• In the afternoon, all the toads are
    on toadstools
• Jenny is   a toad
• So in the afternoon, Jenny is
    on a toadstool

(red bugs [dots] in bush)

berry bush

(red)

Where is Rod the red
bug in the afternoon?

• In the afternoon, all the red bugs are
    in the berry bush
• Rod is   a red bug
• So in the afternoon, Rod is
    in the berry bush

A

1.

The bees chased us.

Clarabelle hid (preposition and object).

Goober hid (preposition and object).

I hid (preposition and object).

2.

Everybody made something.

Molly made (child's choice).

Bleep made (child's choice).

I made (child's choice).

3.

Everybody wrote a letter.

Liz wrote to (child's choice).

Owen wrote to (child's choice).

I wrote to (child's choice).

(picture based on any sentence)	(picture based on any sentence)

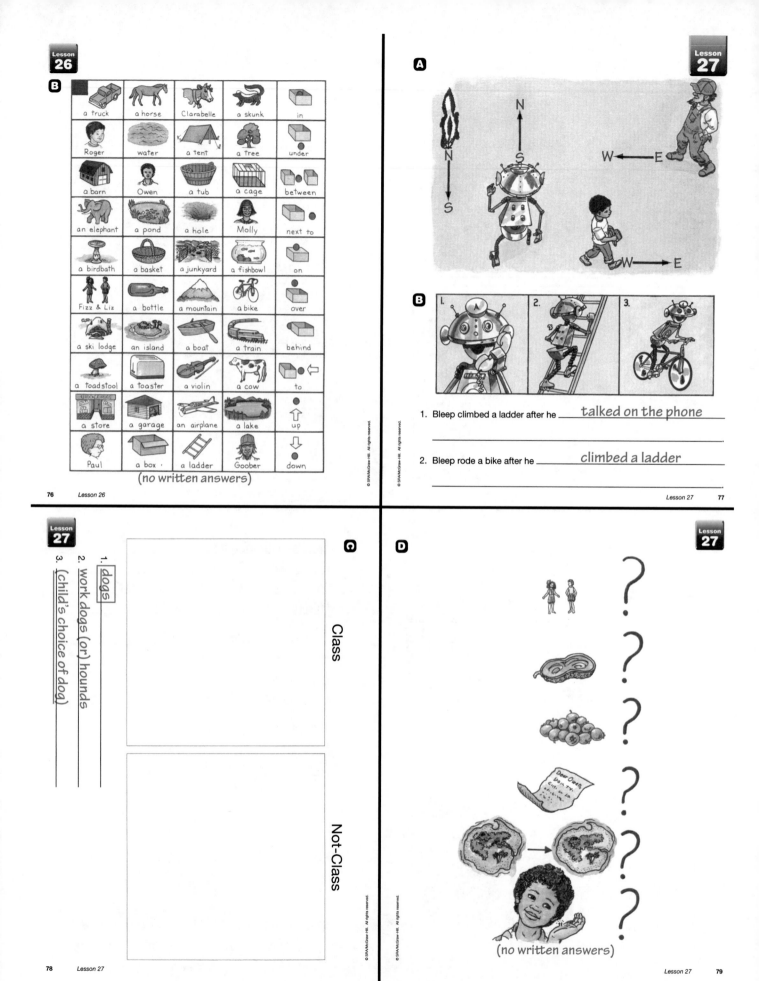

B

a truck	a horse	Clarabelle	a skunk	in
Roger	water	a tent	a tree	under
a barn	Owen	a tub	a cage	between
an elephant	a pond	a hole	Molly	next to
a birdbath	a basket	a junkyard	a fishbowl	on
Fizz & Liz	a bottle	a mountain	a bike	over
a ski lodge	an island	a boat	a train	behind
a toadstool	a toaster	a violin	a cow	to
a store	a garage	an airplane	a lake	up
Paul	a box	a ladder	Goober	down

(no written answers)

A

B

1. Bleep climbed a ladder after he _____talked on the phone_____

_____

2. Bleep rode a bike after he _____climbed a ladder_____

_____

C

1. _dogs_
2. work dogs (or) hounds
3. (child's choice of dog)

Class	Not-Class

D

?
?
?
?
?
?

(no written answers)

20

1. Clarabelle jumped into a pond after she ___climbed a tree___

2. Clarabelle climbed a tree after she ___drove a truck___

oak tree · lily pads

A. Where is Bonnie the bluebird in the afternoon?

   1. In the afternoon, all the bluebirds are in the oak tree.

   2. Bonnie is a ___bluebird___.

   3. So in the afternoon, ___Bonnie is in the oak tree___.

B. Where is Fran the frog in the afternoon?

   1. In the afternoon, all the frogs are ___on lily pads___.

   2. Fran is a ___a frog___.

   3. So in the afternoon, ___Fran is on a lily pad___.

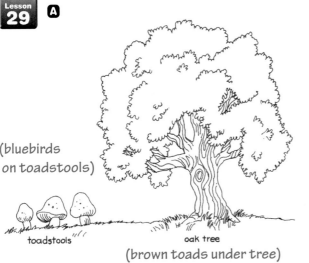

(bluebirds on toadstools)

toadstools · oak tree

(brown toads under tree)

A. Where is Tammy the toad in the morning?

   1. In the morning, all the toads are ___under the oak tree___

   2. Tammy is a ___toad___.

   3. So in the morning, Tammy is ___under the oak tree___

B. Where is Bonnie the bluebird in the morning?

   1. In the morning, all the bluebirds are ___on toadstools___

   2. Bonnie is a ___bluebird___.

   3. So in the morning, Bonnie is ___on a toadstool___

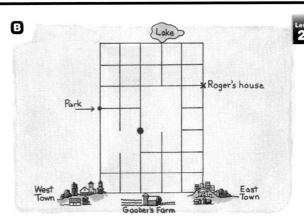

Lake · Roger's house · Park · West Town · East Town · Goober's Farm

1. To go to Roger's house, you go __2__ miles ___north___

   Then you go __3__ miles ___east___.

2. To go to West Town, you go __3__ miles ___south___.

   Then you go __2__ miles ___west___.

C (no written answers)

Collie · Saint Bernard

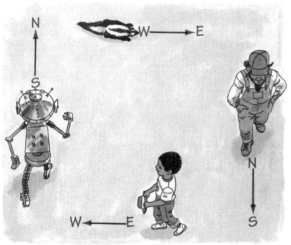

(blue line from kennel to dot between F and C)

(brown line from kennel to level spot at F; then zigzag; then south)

N
W
E
S
C
F

Rescue Station

SOUTH LODGE
Kitchen

Lesson 30 — Test 3

Test Score

A

| skipped | catch | played | rope |

| The boys played catch. |
| The girls jumped rope. |
| (Optional: Students skip a line and write both |
| sentences again.) |

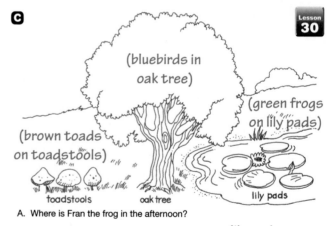

N
S
W E

N
S
W E

(bluebirds in oak tree)

(green frogs on lily pads)

(brown toads on toadstools)

toadstools   oak tree   lily pads

A. Where is Fran the frog in the afternoon?

1. In the afternoon, all the frogs are ___on lily pads___

2. Fran is a ___frog___.

3. So in the afternoon, Fran is ___on a lily pad___

B. Where is Bonnie the bluebird in the afternoon?

1. In the afternoon, all the bluebirds are ___in the oak tree___

2. Bonnie is a ___bluebird___

3. So in the afternoon, Bonnie is ___in the oak tree___

C. Where is Tammy the toad in the afternoon?

1. In the afternoon, all the toads are ___on toadstools___

2. Tammy is a ___toad___

3. So in the afternoon, Tammy is ___on a toadstool___

(sentence of the form:
character 1 got mad at character 2)

(picture showing character 2
doing something annoying)

(Lesson 31 on lined paper)

Everybody ate and ate.
Dud ate (child's choice).
Molly ate (child's choice).
I ate (child's choice).

Everybody looked for something.
Dot looked for (child's choice).
Fizz and Lizz looked for (child's choice).
I looked for (child's choice).

Everybody got mad.
Dot got mad at (child's choice).
Goober got mad at (child's choice).
I got mad at (child's choice).

A

ball	end
go	ant
dig	candy
fill	

1. ant
2. ball
3. candy
4. dig
5. end
6. fill
7. go

B

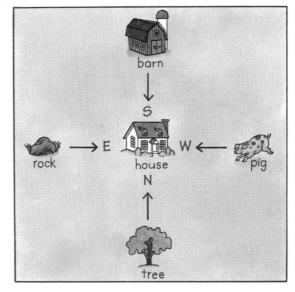

1. The house is west of _the pig_ .
2. The house is north of _the tree_ .
3. The house is east of _the rock_ .
4. The house is south of _the barn_ .

C

Class

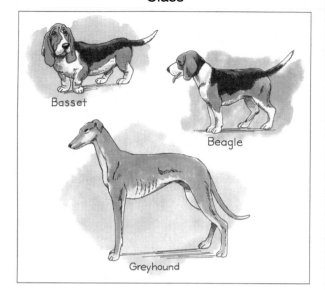

_3_ hounds

_4_ fast-running hounds

_2_ dogs

_1_ animals

D

N

Ⓒ

Ⓑ ← (blue)

← (blue)

Ⓕ

(brown) →

W

Rescue Station

E

SOUTH LODGE

Kitchen

S

A

line	help
ground	kitchen
it	jumps
moon	

1. _ground_
2. _help_
3. _it_
4. _jumps_
5. _kitchen_
6. _line_
7. _moon_

B

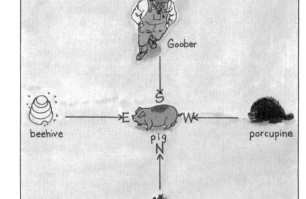

Goober

S

beehive E — W porcupine

pig

N

skunk

1. The pig is south of _Goober_ .

2. The pig is north of _the skunk_ .

3. The pig is west of _the porcupine_ .

4. The pig is east of _the beehive_ .

Class

_3_ work dogs

_1_ animals

_4_ work dogs with ears that stand straight up

_2_ dogs

A

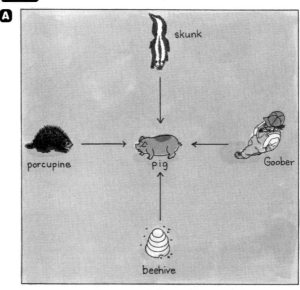

1. The pig is east of _the porcupine_ .

2. The pig is north of _the beehive_ .

3. The pig is west of _Goober_ .

4. The pig is south of _the skunk_ .

B

1. Goober _went to sleep_
   after he milked a cow.

2. Goober _took a bath_
   after he played the violin.

3. Goober _milked a cow_
   after he took a bath.

(Lesson 34 on lined paper)
Everybody jumped over something.
Mrs. Hudson jumped over (child's choice).
Goober jumped over (child's choice).
I jumped over (child's choice).

C

The pigs

1. My brother and my sister had pet pigs. ~~They~~ just loved to roll around in the mud.

the glass

2. We always kept a glass on top of the refrigerator. We kept ~~it~~ full of water.

A

helpful	knock
jumpy	gate
farmer	landed
inside	

1. <u>farmer</u>
2. <u>gate</u>
3. <u>helpful</u>
4. <u>inside</u>
5. <u>jumpy</u>
6. <u>knock</u>
7. <u>landed</u>

B

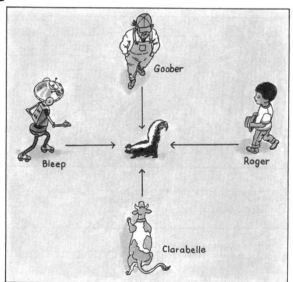

1. The skunk is north of <u>Clarabelle</u>
2. The skunk is east of <u>Bleep</u>
3. The skunk is west of <u>Roger</u>
4. The skunk is south of <u>Goober</u>

C

A.
This thing is in the class of bikes.

<u>1, 2, 3, 4, 5, 7</u>

B.
This thing is in the class of black bikes.

<u>2, 5, 7</u>

C.
This thing is in the class of black bikes with a flat front tire.

<u>3, 5, 7</u>

D.
This thing is in the class of black bikes with a flat front tire and

<u>a flat back tire</u>

1.

2.

3.

4.

5.

6.

7.

8.

D

My brother and sister

1. My brother and my sister had pet pigs. <u>They</u> just loved to roll around in the mud.

the refrigerator

2. We always kept a glass on top of the refrigerator. We kept **X** full of water.

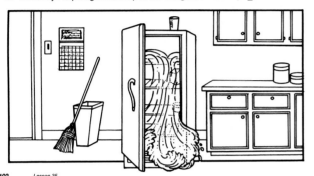

A

jaws	oldest
lake	kitten
nothing	meaning
ice	

1. <u>ice</u>
2. <u>jaws</u>
3. <u>kitten</u>
4. <u>lake</u>
5. <u>meaning</u>
6. <u>nothing</u>
7. <u>oldest</u>

B

The pond is south.

The pond is east.

The pond is north.

The pond is west.

C

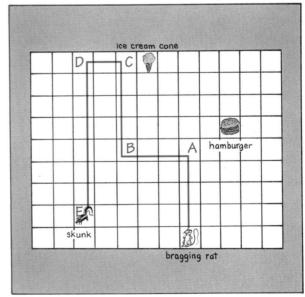

Step A.   4 squares north

Step B.   3 squares west

Step C.   4 squares north

Step D.   2 squares west

Step E.   7 squares south

The bragging rat ended up at the ____ <u>skunk</u> ____.

Lesson 36

Mother

Mother held Baby Sarah as ~~she~~ drank from a baby bottle.

D

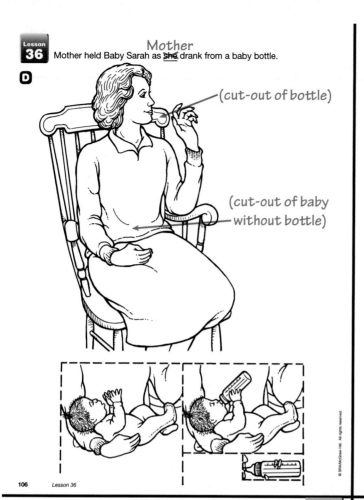

(cut-out of bottle)

(cut-out of baby without bottle)

(Lesson 37 on lined paper)
Everybody played.
Dot played with (child's choice).
Zelda played with (child's choice).
I played with (child's choice).

Lesson 37

A

rat

beehive

hot dog

A   B

D   C

skunk

apple

Step A.	3 squares north
Step B.	1 square east
Step C.	1 square south
Step D.	3 squares west
Step E.	4 squares north

The skunk ended up at the <u>rat</u> _____.

Lesson 37

B

4.   3.   2.   1.

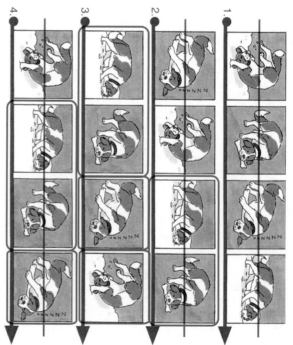

C

The car

1. Our car made a dust cloud. ❌ floated away.

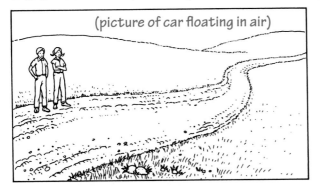
(picture of car floating in air)

The car

2. A frog was on top of the car. ❌ had big black spots all over.

(big black spots on car)

D

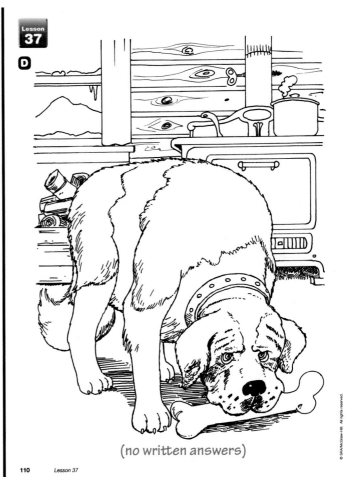

(no written answers)

A

restful	question
pound	until
older	thing
something	

1. older
2. pound
3. question
4. restful
5. something
6. thing
7. until

B

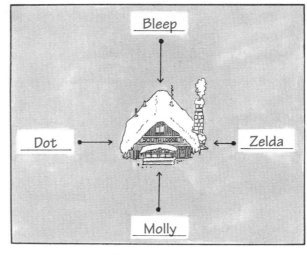

29

C

We had a fence next to the barn. Our dog jumped over ~~X~~. _the barn_

(picture of a dog jumping over barn)

D

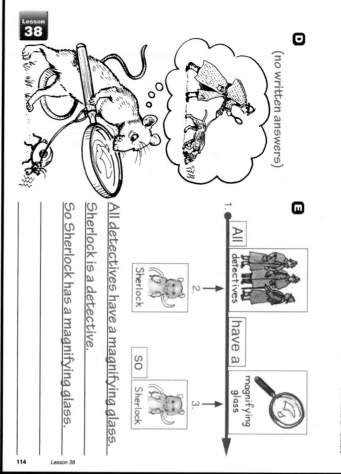

(no written answers)

E

1.

All detectives have a magnifying glass

Sherlock → 2.

SO Sherlock → 3.

All detectives have a magnifying glass.

Sherlock is a detective.

So Sherlock has a magnifying glass.

A

wishful	ugly
time	x-ray
zoo	van
yawning	

1. _time_
2. _ugly_
3. _van_
4. _wishful_
5. _x-ray_
6. _yawning_
7. _zoo_

B

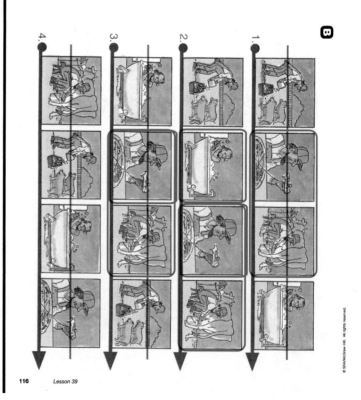

30

C My brothers

My brothers had dogs. They loved to carry a bone around in their mouth.

(picture of a bone in each boy's mouth)

D

1. went into

(no written answers)

2.   3.

Sherlock   Bartha   Goober   Wise Old Rat

Test 4

A

| chair | woman | sitting | painting |

	The woman was painting a chair.
	The man was sitting in a chair.
	(Optional: Students skip a line and write
	both sentences again.)

Lesson 40—Test 4

Test Score ☐

B

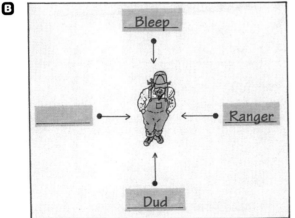

Bleep

Ranger

Dud

Goober is north.

Goober is west.

Goober is south.

Dud   Ranger   Bleep

C

1. Owen ate bananas after he put (the) note in (the) bottle *a* ... *a*

2. Owen went swimming after he put (the) bottle in the *a* ocean (water)

3. Owen put a note in the bottle after he wrote (the note) *it*

D

1. boys   (children)
2. (animals)   cows
3. (fruit)   apples

31

A

| rode | horse | bike | girl |

| The boy rode a bike. |
| The girl rode a horse. |
| (Optional: Students skip a line and write both sentences again.) |

B

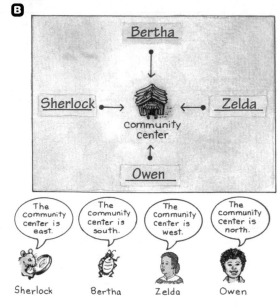

Bertha

Sherlock → community center ← Zelda

Owen

| The community center is east. | The community center is south. | The community center is west. | The community center is north. |

Sherlock   Bertha   Zelda   Owen

C

the pie

1. Aunt Mary put her pie near the stool and Wilber sat on it.

(picture of boy sitting on pie)

little Billy

2. Uncle Henry talked to little Billy as he shaved.

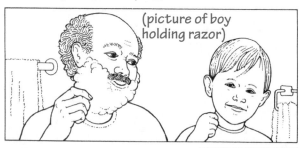

(picture of boy holding razor)

D

(picture of completed circle of pine needles)

A

| mopped | washed | dishes | floor |

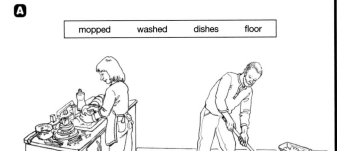

	The woman washed the dishes.
	The man mopped the floor.
	(Optional: Students skip a line and write both sentences again.)

B

the boys

When the boys petted the dogs, they wagged their tails.

(picture of tail on each boy)

C

(no written answers)

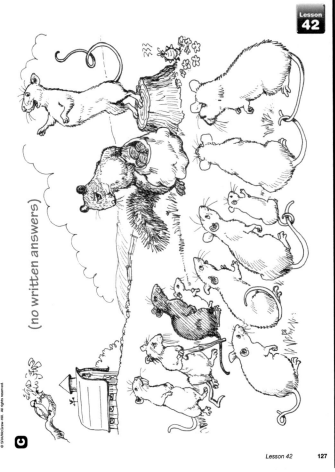

A

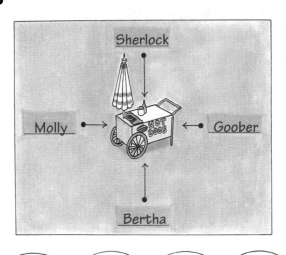

Sherlock

Molly   Goober

Bertha

| The hot dog stand is south. | The hot dog stand is east. | The hot dog stand is north. | The hot dog stand is west. |
| Sherlock | Molly | Bertha | Goober |

(Lined paper for Lesson 43.)
Everybody hid.
Goober hid (location of child's choice).
Bertha hid (location of child's choice).
I hid (location of child's choice).

B

The children

The children caught butterflies. They had orange wings.

(picture of orange wings on children)

A

went swimming	stood on a stump	Sherlock	Zelda	painted a picture	Bertha

1.
Sherlock went swimming.

2. Zelda painted a picture.

3. Bertha stood on a stump.

B

Where is Fred the frog in the afternoon?

a. In the afternoon, all the _frogs_ are on lily pads.

b. Fred is a _frog_.

c. So in the afternoon, _Fred is on a lily pad_.

34

Lesson 44

(no written answers)

132   Lesson 44

Lesson 45

A

| its | gray | scratched | chased | rabbit | ear |

| The black dog chased a rabbit. |
| The gray dog scratched its ear. |
| (Optional: Students skip a line and write both sentences again.) |

Lesson 45   133

Lesson 45

B

| Goober | Paul | painted a pot | fed the pigs | sat on an apple | Fizz and Liz |

1. Paul painted a pot.

2. Goober fed the pigs.

3. Fizz and Liz sat on an apple.

134   Lesson 45

Lesson 45

C

The girls had pet goats. One of them had very long horns.

(picture of long horns on one of the girls)

Lesson 45   135

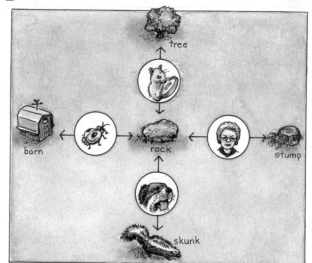

D

Where is Sherlock after dinner?

barn

1. After dinner, all the rats are _in the barn_ .

2. Sherlock _is a rat_ .

3. So after dinner, _Sherlock is in the barn_ .

A

tree

barn   rock   stump

skunk

1. Bertha said, "The rock is _east_ of me and the _barn_ is _west_ of me."

2. Mrs. Hudson said, "The rock is _west_ of me and the _stump_ is _east_ of me."

3. Sherlock said, "The rock is _south_ of me and the _tree_ is _north_ of me."

(Lined paper for Lesson 46.)
Everybody bought something.
Owen bought (child's choice).
Mrs. Hudson bought (child's choice).
I bought (child's choice).

B

played in the snow   kissed Bleep   painted a paddle

1. Paul painted a paddle.

2. Dud played in the snow.

3. Molly kissed Bleep.

C

It's very difficult to understand.

3

1

2

A

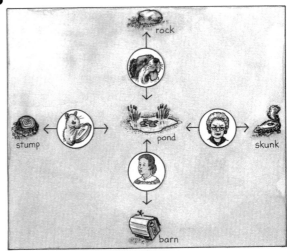

rock
stump   pond   skunk
barn

1. Zelda said, "The pond is __north__ of me and the __barn__ is __south__ of me."

2. Sherlock said, "The pond is __east__ of me and the __stump__ is __west__ of me."

3. Mrs. Hudson said, "The pond is __west__ of me and the __skunk__ is __east__ of me."

B

| played a violin | took a bath | held his hat |

1. Goober took a bath.

2. Roger held his hat.

3. Molly played a violin.

C

1. The boys played with dogs. The dogs had short tails.   *They*

2. The girls went in boats. The boats were made of wood.   *They*

3. The truck went up a hill. The truck had a flat tire.   *It*

(picture of one of the items)

A

ceiling	short	tall	painting

	The tall woman was painting the ceiling.
	The short woman was painting the wall.
	(Optional: Students skip a line and write both sentences again.)

B

Bleep Dud Zelda Mrs. Hudson	rolled in the mud sat on Roger played in the snow chased a skunk said silly things

1. Bleep said silly things.
2. Dud played in the snow.
3. Zelda (Mrs. Hudson) (child's choice of predicate).

(picture of sentence 3)

C

Bolly will dot fide it fuddy.

I fixed myself.

Molly will not find it funny.

I fixed byself.

A

ate	spotted	corn	white	goat	grass

	The white goat ate grass.
	The spotted goat ate corn.
	(Optional: Students skip a line and write both sentences again.)

B

Bleep, are you almost finished?

Blurp. ~~Yes.~~

Lesson 50—Test 5

Test Score ▢

A

Molly	ran home
Bertha	sat on a cake
Owen	kissed Goober
Mrs. Hudson	fixed Bleep
	fed the pigs
	picked up Owen

1. Molly fixed Bleep.

2. Bertha ran home.

   Owen
3. (Mrs. Hudson) (child's choice of predicate).

(picture of sentence 3)

B

N

W   E

S

stump

skunk

barn

rock

pond

1. Zelda said, "The skunk is _east_ of me and the _barn_ is _west_ of me."

2. Molly said, "The skunk is _north_ of me and the _pond_ is _south_ of me."

3. Bertha said, "The skunk is _west_ of me and the _rock_ is _east_ of me."

A

| young | leaves | chopped | raked |

	The old man chopped logs.
	The young man raked leaves.
	(Optional: Students skip a line and write both sentences again.)

B

1. _____ Dud ate a ham bone _____

after he played in the snow.

2. Dud ___went swimming after he ate a ham bone___

_____.

C

1. Aunt Martha pulled a turnip out of the dirt.

It

~~The turnip~~ tasted good.

2. The ranger led the dogs toward the mountains.

They

~~The mountains~~ were covered with snow.

(picture of one of the items)

D

Anybody who has squash
on their breath ate squash.
The bluebirds _have squash on_
their breath
So _the bluebirds ate squash_

A

1. ____ Bleep read a book after he fed a cat. ____

_____

2. ____ Bleep kissed Molly after he read a book. ____

_____

Lesson 52

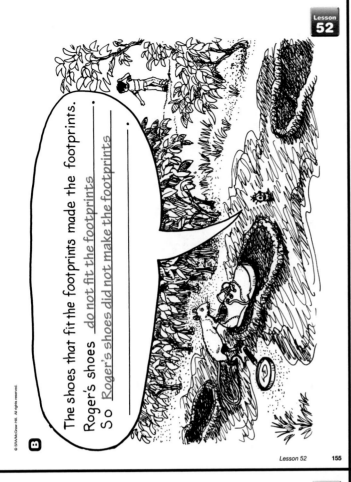

B

The shoes that fit the footprints made the footprints.
Roger's shoes _do not fit the footprints_
So _Roger's shoes did not make the footprints_

Lesson 53

A

zoo

friends

class

family

elephants   lions   tigers

bears   monkeys   giraffes   parrots

Dear _(child's choice)_ ,

Yesterday, I went to the _____ zoo _____ with my
(choice of friends,
~~family, class~~) . We saw _(child's choice of animal_s)
(child's choice of , and _(child's choice of animal_s)
animals)
My favorite animals were the _(child's choice of animals)_

I hope that I can go back to the _____ zoo _____ soon.

From,

_____ (child's name) _____

Lesson 53

B

1. _Goober took a bath after he fed the pigs._

2. _Goober played a violin after he took a bath._

Lesson 53

C

The shoes that smell of squash went in squash.
Goober's shoes _smell of squash_
So _Goober's shoes went in squash_

(no written answers)

A

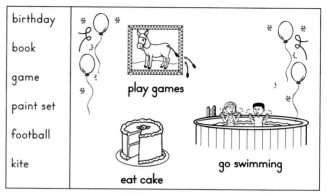

birthday

book

game

paint set

football

kite

play games

eat cake

go swimming

Dear _(child's choice)_ ,

    Next week, I will be _____(child's choice)_____ years old. I am going to

have a _____birthday_____ party. My friends and I

will _(child's choice of activities)_ and

(child's choice of activities) . The birthday present I

want most is a _____(child's choice)_____ . I hope I get it.

    From,

    (child's name)

B

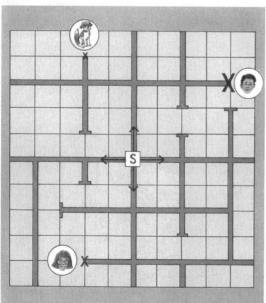

1. To go to Molly, you go __4__ miles ___south___ and __2__ miles

   ___west___ .

2. To go to Owen, you go __3__ miles ___north___ and __4__ miles

   ___east___ .

C

1. Three ladies picked berries.
   They
   ~~The berries~~ were blue.

2. Our chicken laid an egg.
   It
   ~~The egg~~ was no bigger than a stone.

3. We used a shovel to plant the flower.
   It
   ~~The flower~~ grew all summer long.

(picture of item 3 —
a shovel growing
very large)

A

school	
go for walks	
my grandma's	
the park	

dog   cat   fish   parrot   turtle   hamster   snake   bunny

Dear _(child's choice)_,

The pet that I would like the most is a _____ _(child's choice)_.

I would name my pet _(child's choice)_, and I would take care of my ___pet___ _(or type of pet)_. We would have a lot of fun together.

I would take my pet to _(child's choice)_ and to _(child's choice)_.

I would love my ___pet___ _(or type of pet)_, and my pet would love me.

From,

(child's name)

B

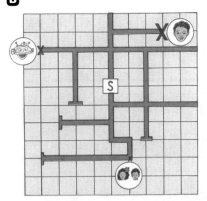

1. To go to Bleep, you go _2_ miles ___north___ and _4_ miles ___west___.

2. To go to Owen, you go _3_ miles ___north___ and _3_ miles ___east___.

C

All

2.   3.

a. (good)   bad
b. good   (bad)
c. (good)   bad

D

1. Three little boys picked strawberries. They were as big as apples.

Henry

Zelda

2. Before the children pulled up the tulips, my sister watered them with the hose.

Zelda

Henry

43

A

1.
2.
3.

1. <u>Sherlock went swimming after he stood on a</u>
   <u>stump.</u>
2. <u>Sherlock went to sleep after he went</u>
   <u>swimming.</u>

B

1. Zelda drove a van to the picnic.	reports	(does not report)
2. Three people sat at a picnic table.	(reports)	does not report
3. Everybody was going to swim later that day.	reports	(does not report)
4. Roger wore a hat.	(reports)	does not report
5. Zelda ate more than anybody else.	reports	(does not report)
6. A van was close to the picnic tables.	(reports)	does not report
7. Zelda sat next to Mrs. Hudson.	(reports)	does not report

C

Donna and her mother watched the tiny spiders. They were upside down in their web.

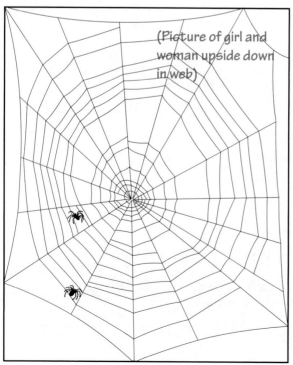

(Picture of girl and woman upside down in web)

A

1. Sherlock ate too much corn.	reports	(does not report)
2. Bertha was mad at Sherlock.	reports	(does not report)
3. Cyrus pulled a large sack.	(reports)	does not report
4. Bertha played a violin.	(reports)	does not report
5. The wise old rat was dirty.	reports	(does not report)
6. The sack was full of hazelnuts.	reports	(does not report)
7. The wise old rat was wet.	(reports)	does not report

B

ate a burger
sat under a tree
drove a van
went fishing
ate watermelon
sat on a table
ate pie

	Molly ate a burger.
	Roger sat under a tree.
	Zelda ate pie.
	Mrs. Hudson ate watermelon.

} (child chooses one)

C

1. This lump goes in the bag.
2. I run on the track.
3. The stumps are in a stack.

D

Team A   1.

Team B   2.

Team C   3.

1. A: Zelda went jogging after she sat on a stump.
   B: Zelda ate an apple after she went jogging.
   C: Zelda ate an apple after she rode a horse.

2. A: Zelda rode a horse after she went jogging.
   B: Zelda rode a horse after she sat on a stump.
   C: Zelda went jogging after she sat on a stump.

(Answers vary by team.)

A

washed	mopped	read	painted
book	window	floor	piano

Bleep mopped the floor.
Molly washed (the, a) window.
Paul painted (the, a) piano.
Zelda read (the, a) book.

B

(no written answers — Pictures are guide for oral story.)

rode	ate	played	jumped	read
rope	banana	book	violin	bike

Mrs. Hudson rode (the, a) bike.
Zelda jumped rope.
Molly ate (the, a) banana.
Goober played (the, a) violin.

(Bleep-talk with
short-a word(s)
written with
short u)

(Molly's
response)

Lesson 60—Test 6

Test Score [ ]

A

striped	bike	rode	patch
pants	small	shirt	wore

(any order)

The man rode a small bike.
The man wore a striped shirt.
The man had a patch on his pants.

B

căn	cake	corn	răt	tăck	bend

C

1. Bleep was holding a can of paint. (reports) does not report

2. Only part of the fence was painted. (reports) does not report

3. Bleep did not hear Molly. reports (does not report)

4. Molly is getting irritated with Bleep. reports (does not report)

5. Molly's car door was open. (reports) does not report

6. Molly called for Bleep's help. (reports) does not report

A

Sherlock said, "The pond is **east** of me and the
barn is **west** of me."

Goober said, "The pond is **south** of me and the
skunk is **north** of me."

Bleep said, "The pond is **west** of me and the
house is **east** of me."

Bertha said, "The pond is **north** of me and the
stump is **south** of me."

B

wore	collar	spots	chewed	bone

(any order)

The dog wore a collar.
The dog had spots.
The dog chewed a big bone.

C

It Folds Up

It was regular-sized with two full-sized wheels.

Then it folded up to the size of a book.

She said "I got the idea when I talked to him."

Molly Henderson

Angelo

accordion

A Bike Folds Up
The bike was regular-sized with two full-sized wheels. Then the bike folded up to the size of a book. Molly Henderson said, "I got the idea when I talked to Angelo, the accordion player."

A

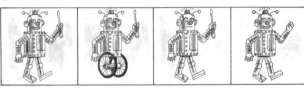

legs	wheels	smiled	held	screwdriver

(any order)

The robot smiled.
The robot held a screwdriver.
The robot had legs.

B (3 of 4 below)

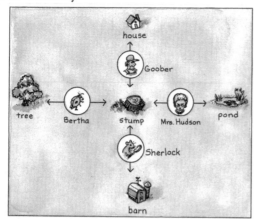

Bertha said, "The stump is _east_ of me and the
tree is _west_ of me."

Goober said, "The stump is _south_ of me and the
house is _north_ of me."

Mrs. Hudson said, "The stump is _west_ of me and the
pond is _east_ of me."

Sherlock said, "The stump is _north_ of me and the
barn is _south_ of me."

D (Ideas:)   the beach   the sand
Linda Carry was at ~~it~~. She was digging in ~~it~~.
the (ten gold) coins
She found ~~them~~. She sold ~~them~~.

(ten gold) coins

beach	rooster	gold coins	bushes	trees
ten	sand	turkeys	money	

A

1. Mrs. Hudson rode her bike.   (Ideas:)

2. Mrs. Hudson _went into her house after she rode her bike_ .

3. Mrs. Hudson _took a shower after she went into her house_ .

after	shower	house	took	she

B

hair	glasses	smiled	long	wore

(any order)

The woman wore glasses.
The woman had long hair.
The woman smiled.

C   (no written answers)

D

(no written answers)

E

1. B is not the safe landing place because B is not

   south of the hill .

2. C is not the safe landing place because C is not

   north of the lake .

A

| she | stood | wore | brush |
| chair | hat | used | |

The woman painted a wall.
(next 3 ideas in any order)
She stood on a chair.
She wore a hat.
She used a (paint) brush.

B

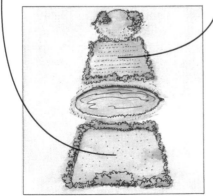

C

apples

pizza

burgers

ice cream

corn on the cob

macaroni and cheese

read a book

play in the park

draw

(Date)

Dear (child's choice)

Here are a few of my favorite things. My favorite things to eat
are (choice of food) and (choice of food). My favorite things to do
are (choice of activity) and (choice of activity). My favorite people are
(choice of person) and (choice of person).

From,

(child's name)

A

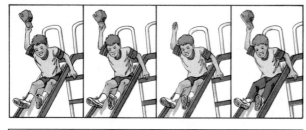

slid	slide	down	boy	shorts	smiled	held

	The boy slid down the slide.
	(next 3 items in any order)
	He smiled.
	He held a hat.
	He wore shorts.

B

(no written answers)

C

three wishes — a vacation — a castle — a skateboard — a friend — a horse — a magic wand — money

_____(Date)_____

Dear (child's choice)

This is what I would wish for if I had _three wishes_. First, I would wish for (child's choice) Next, I would wish for (child's choice)

Last, I would wish for (child's choice)

From,

(child's name)

A

Circle **reports** if a sentence reports on what the picture shows.
Circle **does not report** if the sentence does not report on what the picture shows.

1. The three men were brothers.   reports   (does not report)
2. Three men fished from a boat.   (reports)   does not report
3. The men were going to have fish for dinner.   reports   (does not report)
4. A big dog stood in the boat.   reports   (does not report)
5. All the men wore hats.   (reports)   does not report
6. One man held a net.   (reports)   does not report
7. One fishing pole bent down toward the water. (reports)   does not report
8. A large fish was on the end of the line.   reports   (does not report)

B   Circle the part of each sentence that names.

1. (The old man) went to the store.
2. (The man and the boy) went to the store.
3. (The horse) jumped over the fence.

C

●Name
1. He ate a green apple.
2. Alice found a dime.
3. David took a walk in the park.
●(Student's Name)
1. He ate a green apple.
2. Alice found a dime.
3. David took a walk in the park.

D

1.	The baby deer	stood next to the mother deer.
2.	A rabbit	hopped over a log.
3.	A frog	sat on a log.

E

1.	All vehicles can move.
2.	A car is a vehicle.
3.	So a car can move

A

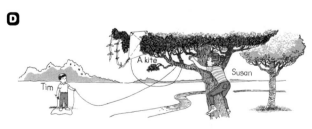

Circle **reports** if a sentence reports on what the picture shows.
Circle **does not report** if the sentence does not report on what the picture shows.

1. The children had been camping for three days.   reports   (does not report)
2. A girl gave something to a dog.   (reports)   does not report
3. The girls liked chicken.   reports   (does not report)
4. Two girls and a boy sat at a picnic table.   (reports)   does not report
5. Cups and plates were on the table.   (reports)   does not report
6. The boy petted the dog.   reports   (does not report)
7. The boy wanted to go home.   reports   (does not report)

B   Circle the part of each sentence that names.

1. (Two girls) are eating ice cream.
2. (A black cat) ran under the fence.
3. (A man and a woman) sat on the porch.

C

●Name
1. Alex got a nice gift.
2. My sister is ten years old.
3. She fell asleep.
●(Student's Name)
1. Alex got a nice gift.
2. My sister is ten years old.
3. She fell asleep.

D

1.	Tim	held the kite string.
2.	Susan	climbed the tree.
3.	A kite	was stuck in a tree.

E

1.	All fish have fins.
2.	A bass is a fish.
3.	So a bass has fins

A   Circle the part of each sentence that names.

1. (A little girl) ate two apples.   3. (A kite) went high in the sky.

2. (A cow and a horse) ate grass.   4. (My brother) washed the dishes.

B

A sad clown   A monkey

Kathy   A bear

1.	A sad clown	rode a bicycle.
2.	A bear	juggled three balls.
3.	A monkey	walked on the rope.
4.	Kathy	laughed at the clown.

C

1.	Every worker uses tools.
2.	A plumber is a worker.
3.	So a plumber uses tools

Lesson 67   **201**

202   Lesson 68

A   In each blank, write the word that tells what people did.

What people do	What people did
1. burn	burned
2. fill	filled
3. push	pushed
4. lick	licked
5. start	started
6. scratch	scratched

B   Put the name of a vehicle in the blanks.

1.	All vehicles can move.
2.	A _(any vehicle)_ is a vehicle.
3.	So a _(same vehicle)_ can move.

truck	boat	train	car	plane	bike

C

1. The little cats were in bed.

2. They were in bed.

3. Five birds sat in the tree.

4. A dog chased a cat.

A   In each blank, write the word that tells what people did.

What people do	What people did
1. jump	jumped
2. pull	pulled
3. play	played
4. push	pushed
5. spill	spilled
6. trick	tricked

B   In each blank, write the word that tells what people did.

1. find	found	6. buy	bought	11. dig	dug
2. give	gave	7. find	found	12. buy	bought
3. buy	bought	8. dig	dug	13. have	had
4. dig	dug	9. have	had	14. give	gave
5. have	had	10. give	gave	15. find	found

C

1.	Every building has a roof.
2.	A _(any building)_ is a building.
3.	So _(same building)_ has a roof

a church	a house	a school	a store	a shed

Lesson 69   **203**

204   Lesson 70

A In each blank, write the word that tells what people did.

1. give   _gave_
2. dig   _dug_
3. find   _found_
4. have   _had_
5. buy   _bought_

6. dig   _dug_
7. find   _found_
8. buy   _bought_
9. give   _gave_
10. have   _had_

B Fix up the sentences so they tell what people did.

1. Alicia ~~was fixing~~ her bike.   _fixed_
2. The girl ~~was talking~~ loudly.   _talked_
3. Miss Cook ~~is finding~~ her keys.   _found_
4. Her grandmother ~~is smiling~~ at the baby.   _smiled_
5. Mr. Howard ~~was buying~~ a picture.   _bought_

C Circle the part that names. Underline the part that tells more.

1. (Three tall girls) sat on a horse.
2. (They) rode the horse across the field.
3. (Their horse) jumped over a fence.
4. (A girl and her horse) went across a stream.
5. (She) rested under a tree.

D

1.	Every bird has wings.
2.	A (any bird) is a bird.
3.	So a (same bird) has wings .

a robin	a sparrow	a bluebird	a hawk

A Circle the part that names. Underline the part that tells more.

1. (That sad clown) rode on a bicycle.
2. (He) had a monkey on his head.
3. (The monkey) went over to Sam.
4. (Clowns and monkeys) fell down.
5. (They) made people laugh.

B Fix up the sentences so they tell what people did.

1. He ~~is giving~~ her a kiss.   _gave_
2. We ~~were having~~ fun.   _had_
3. Boys and girls ~~were buying~~ lunch.   _bought_
4. The man ~~is painting~~ the house.   _painted_
5. Josh ~~was finding~~ his socks.   _found_
6. Miss Clark ~~is digging~~ in the garden.   _dug_

C Fill in the blanks with **He** or **She**.
Remember to start each sentence with a capital.

1. The girl was running.
2. My grandfather read a book.
3. Mary painted the wall.
4. Bill walked home.
5. My brother woke up.
6. His mother washed her hands.

1. _She_ was running.
2. _He_ read a book.
3. _She_ painted the wall.
4. _He_ walked home.
5. _He_ woke up.
6. _She_ washed her hands.

A

1. (A boy and his dad) went to a baseball game.
2. (They) ate lots of popcorn.
3. (The boy) caught a baseball.
4. (One baseball player) wrote his name on the ball.
5. (Yesterday) was a wonderful day.

B Fill in the blanks with **He** or **She**.

1. His sister won the race.
2. Her father went to the park.
3. A tall boy washed the car.
4. The young woman fixed the bike.

1. _She_ won the race.
2. _He_ went to the park.
3. _He_ washed the car.
4. _She_ fixed the bike.

C Fix up the sentences so they tell what people did.

1. Two children ~~are washing~~ the car.   _washed_
2. He ~~is spelling~~ a hard word.   _spelled_
3. Wendy ~~is having~~ a party.   _had_
4. Nick ~~is buying~~ his sister a hat.   _bought_
5. He ~~is finding~~ a pencil.   _found_
6. She ~~was filling~~ the glass with water.   _filled_

D

1.	All trees have leaves.
2.	A (any tree) is a tree.
3.	So a (same tree) has leaves

a maple	a spruce	a pine	a fir	a cedar	a redwood	a birch

Lesson 74

A Fill in the blanks with **He, She** or **It**.

1. That coat was covered with dirt.
2. The rubber ball fell off the table.
3. My mother sat in a chair.
4. This book was very funny.
5. The young woman rode a bike.
6. Susan's game ended early.

1. _____It_____ was covered with dirt.
2. _____It_____ fell off the table.
3. _____She_____ sat in a chair.
4. _____It_____ was very funny.
5. _____She_____ rode a bike.
6. _____It_____ ended early.

B Fix up the sentences so they tell what people did.

1. He ~~was having~~ fun. **had**
2. She ~~is looking~~ at the sky. **looked**
3. Alice ~~was picking~~ apples. **picked**
4. She ~~is buying~~ a dress. **bought**
5. Ann ~~is digging~~ in the sand. **dug**
6. She ~~was folding~~ the paper. **folded**

C Circle the part that names. Underline the part that tells more.

1. (Carla and Tom) rode their bikes to the park.
2. (They) had a picnic with Mary and Beth.
3. (A big dog) took Tom's sandwich.
4. (Rain) started to fall.
5. (The children) went home quickly.

Lesson 74   **209**

Test 7

Lesson 75   Test Score [ ]

A

Circle **reports** if a sentence reports on what the picture shows.
Circle **does not report** if the sentence does not report on what the picture shows.

1. The cowboys were very hungry.	reports	(does not report)
2. Alfred poured soup in a pot.	(reports)	does not report
3. James cooked hot dogs over the fire.	reports	(does not report)
4. All the cowboys wore hats.	(reports)	does not report
5. Jerry used a knife to cut the potato.	(reports)	does not report
6. The horse belonged to Jerry.	reports	(does not report)
7. The soup smelled good.	reports	(does not report)
8. James cooked food over a fire.	(reports)	does not report

210   Lesson 75—Test 7

Lesson 75

B Next to each word, write the word that tells what people did.

What people do	What people did
1. give	gave
2. dig	dug
3. find	found
4. save	saved
5. buy	bought

C Circle the part that names. Underline the part that tells more.

1. (My brother and my sister) were at school.
2. (A glass) fell off the table.
3. (He) liked to look at horses.
4. (A girl and a boy) fixed the fence.
5. (They) painted the room.

D Fix up the sentences so they tell what people did.

1. He ~~was giving~~ me a pen. **gave**
2. He ~~was buying~~ a shirt. **bought**
3. They ~~were picking~~ flowers. **picked**
4. He ~~is filling~~ the glass. **filled**
5. My friend ~~is having~~ a party. **had**
6. A boy ~~is spelling~~ words. **spelled**

Lesson 75—Test 7   **211**

Lesson 76

A In each blank, write the word that tells what people did.

1. wear   *wore*
2. see   *saw*
3. run   *ran*
4. go   *went*
5. sit   *sat*
6. see   saw
7. sit   sat
8. go   went
9. wear   wore
10. run   ran

B Circle the part of each sentence that names.

(Tina and Ginger) wanted to play in the water. (The girls) were wearing jeans. (They) went to the little pool. (The two girls) went into the shallow water. (They) started to splash each other. (Tina and Ginger) were all wet when they left the pool.

C Fill in the blanks with **He, She** or **It**.

1. His big sister parked the car.
2. Ted's car slid down the hill.
3. That movie was interesting.
4. Amanda's brother won the race.
5. The party was fun.

1. _____She_____ parked the car.
2. _____It_____ slid down the hill.
3. _____It_____ was interesting.
4. _____He_____ won the race.
5. _____It_____ was fun.

D Fix up the sentences so they tell what people did.

1. Vanessa ~~is giving~~ the cup to him. **gave**
2. Carlos ~~was jumping~~ over a fence. **jumped**
3. Four children ~~were buying~~ apples. **bought**
4. Mr. Lopez ~~was painting~~ a chair. **painted**

212   Lesson 76

54

A Circle the part of each sentence that names.

(Carla) was in the park. (She) played on the swings. (She) went down a slide. (That tired girl) rested on a bench. (Carla) walked home with her friends.

B In each blank, write the word that tells what people did.

1. see _saw_
2. wear _wore_
3. sit _sat_
4. run _ran_
5. go _went_

6. wear _wore_
7. run _ran_
8. see _saw_
9. go _went_
10. sit _sat_

C Fill in the blanks with **He, She** or **It**.

1. His shirt was covered with dirt.
2. My new pencil fell off the table.
3. A boy sat in a chair.
4. Tamika's book was very funny.
5. A young woman rode a bike.

1. _It_ was covered with dirt.
2. _It_ fell off the table.
3. _He_ sat in a chair.
4. _It_ was very funny.
5. _She_ rode a bike.

D

1.	Every bird has wings.
2.	A (any bird) _is a bird._
3.	_So_ a (same bird) _has wings_

a robin   a crow   a hawk   a chicken

A Fix up the sentences so they tell what people did.

1. Miss Ross ~~is digging~~ holes for the fence posts. _dug_
2. They ~~are filling~~ the box with sand. _filled_
3. My grandfather ~~was starting~~ his car. _started_
4. She ~~was having~~ a party. _had_
5. Justin ~~is buying~~ milk. _bought_
6. The children ~~were cooking~~ eggs. _cooked_

B Circle the part of each sentence that names.

(An old cowboy) rode his horse to town. (The cowboy) wanted to buy a new hat. (He) rode his horse to the clothing store. (He) tied his horse to a post. (The cowboy) went in the store. (He) found a hat he liked.

C Fill in the blanks with **He, She** or **It**.

1. That red plate was broken.
2. Her brother fell down.
3. My sister had a cold.
4. My father's hat was dirty.
5. An airplane flew over the clouds.
6. Her window was open.

1. _It_ was broken.
2. _He_ fell down.
3. _She_ had a cold.
4. _It_ was dirty.
5. _It_ flew over the clouds.
6. _It_ was open.

A Fill in the blanks with **He, She** or **It**.

1. Robert spent all morning cleaning his room. _He_ put his dirty clothes in the laundry basket.
2. My sister went to the park. _She_ played basketball with her friends for two hours.
3. The boat held four people. _It_ had three sails.

B Circle the part of each sentence that names.

(A little boy) found a small box in his yard. (The box) had three beans in it. (The little boy) showed the beans to his sister. (She) told him to plant the beans. (Three plants) grew from the beans. (Those plants) were made of gold.

C Fix up the sentences so they tell what people did.

1. They ~~were going~~ to the store. _went_
2. He ~~is filling~~ the sink with hot water. _filled_
3. My grandmother ~~was fixing~~ her car. _fixed_
4. She ~~is having~~ fun. _had_
5. Jane ~~was buying~~ a new shirt. _bought_
6. A boy ~~is spelling~~ a hard word. _spelled_

A Fill in the blanks with **He, She** or **It**.

1. His mother liked to fix cars. _She_ worked in a car shop.
2. My father stayed home this morning. _He_ read a book.
3. The bus stopped. _It_ ran out of gas.

B Fix up the sentences so they tell what people did.

1. Maria wanted a birthday party.
2. She asked some boys and girls to the party.
3. The boys and girls ~~were giving~~ her some presents. _gave_
4. Everybody ~~was having~~ fun. _had_
5. The children ~~were playing~~ games outside. _played_
6. They ate cake and ice cream.

C Circle the part of each sentence that names.

(Alex) taught his pet monkey to do many tricks. (The monkey) even learned how to ride a bicycle. (Alex) dressed his monkey in a costume one day. (Alex and his monkey) went to the circus. (They) showed a clown their tricks. (The clown) gave the monkey a job in the circus.

Lesson 81

A Fix up the sentences so they tell what people did.

1. They ~~were having~~ **had** fun at the party.
2. Jessica ~~is wearing~~ **wore** a new dress.
3. My brother painted his room.
4. Tom and Al ~~are going~~ **went** home.
5. She parked the car.
6. They ~~were starting~~ **started** to run.

B Circle the part of each sentence that names.

(Wendy) found a dirty old bicycle at the dump. (She) showed it to her brother. (He) told his sister that the bicycle was in very poor shape. (Wendy) worked on the bike every day for a month. (It) looked like a brand new bike when she was done. (She) gave it to her brother for his birthday. (Wendy and her brother) were very happy.

C Fill in the blanks with **He**, **She** or **It**.

1. Jill went ice-skating. **She** skated with her friends on the pond.
2. Her dad slept on the couch. **He** snored loudly.
3. The motorcycle went by us quickly. **It** made a lot of noise.
4. My kite was new. **It** landed in a tree.

Lesson 82

A Fill in the blanks with **He**, **She** or **It**.

1. Jeff spent two hours doing his homework. **He** worked hard.
2. Jane went to the park. **She** sat and watched the ducks.
3. The cake tasted great. **It** had whipped cream on top.

B Put in capitals and periods. Circle the part of each sentence that names.

(A red kite) floated into the sky. (The wind) blew the kite. (Three brown ducks) flew near the kite. (The kite) went behind some clouds. (It) went so high that nobody could see it.

C Circle the sentence that tells the main thing each group did.

1. The cats had long tails.
A cat chewed on a string.
(The cats played with string.)
The string was on the floor.

2. The woman cut the grass.
The family was outside.
Everybody wore a hat.
(The family worked in the yard.)

3. Three men wore coats and hats.
(Three men walked through the snow.)
The snow was cold.
The men wore snow shoes.

Lesson 83

A Put in capitals and periods. Circle the part of each sentence that names.

(A woman) rode on a sled. (Six dogs) pulled the sled. (It) went through the deep snow. (The woman) was very cold. (Her dogs) liked the snow. (They) slept in the snow.

B Make each sentence tell what a person or thing did.

Mark looked for a hidden treasure. He ~~is going~~ **went** into his backyard with a shovel. He ~~was digging~~ **dug** for a long time. His shovel hit something hard. Mark ~~was reaching~~ **reached** into the hole. He pulled something out. He ~~was finding~~ **found** a bone.

Does each sentence tell what a person or thing did? **X X X X**

C Circle the sentence that tells the main thing each group did.

1. A boy swept the floor.
The room was dirty.
(The children cleaned the room.)
The children were standing.

2. All the farmers wore coats.
(The farmers fed the animals.)
All the farmers were in the barn.
The animals were hungry.

3. Four girls sat in chairs.
The girls had plates and glasses.
(Four girls ate a meal.)
The girls sat around the table.

Lesson 84

A Circle the part that names. Underline the part that tells more.

1. (A horse and a goat) were eating grass.
2. (Those hungry animals) ate all the grass.
3. (They) drank water from a pond.
4. (A car and a truck) went by a pond.
5. (They) were very loud.

B Put in capitals and periods. Circle the part of each sentence that names.

(Tom and his brother) went shopping for food. (They) bought four apples and six oranges. (The food) cost less than five dollars. (Tom) gave the clerk five dollars. (The clerk) gave Tom change.

C

Mr. Walters ~~was buying~~ **bought** an apple tree. He dug a hole in his yard. He placed the tree in the hole. He ~~is filling~~ **filled** the hole with dirt. He ~~is watering~~ **watered** the tree. He took good care of the tree.

Do the sentences tell what Mr. Walters did? **X X X**

Lesson 84

D Circle the sentence that tells the main thing each group did.

1.
Three cowboys felt tired.
Two cowboys smiled.
The cowboys looked at the fire.
(Three cowboys cooked supper.)

2.
The animals wore clothing.
(The animals did tricks.)
The animals were inside.
The animals got food for doing well.

Lesson 85—Test 8   **Test Score** [ ]

A Put in capitals and periods. Circle the part of each sentence that names.

(My older sister) took her dog to the park. **H** her dog chased a skunk. **T** the skunk got mad. **I** it made a terrible stink. **M** (my sister) had to wash her dog for hours to get rid of the smell.

B

went   had
My friends ~~are going~~ to the park. They ~~are having~~ a good time. Two girls
                                                    ran
played on the swings. A boy chased a butterfly. A boy and a girl ~~are running~~ in
stayed
the grass. Everybody ~~is staying~~ in the park until the sun went down.

Do the sentences tell what people did? **X X X X**

Lesson 85

C Write the letter of each picture that shows what the sentence says.

| A. | B. | C. | D. |

1. He held a bottle. ___C___
2. A person held a container. _A, B, C, D_
3. She held a container. _B, D_
4. He held a container. _A, C_

D Fill in the blanks with **He, She** or **It.**

1. His shirt was red and blue. ___It___ had stripes.
2. My mother helped me do my homework. ___She___ is very good at math.
3. His brother is one year old. ___He___ can almost walk.

Lesson 85—Test 8   **223**

Lesson 86

A Put in capitals and periods. Circle the part of each sentence that names.

(Sandy and her dog) went for a walk. **T** they went to the park. **A** a cat ran in front of them. the (dog) started to chase the cat. the (cat) ran up a tree. (Sandy) took her dog home.

B Circle the part that names. Underline the part that tells more.

1. (My best friend and my sister) helped me.
2. (She) had two dollars.
3. (My little sister) was sick.
4. (The horse) fell over.
5. (He) saw a big bird next to the house.
6. (A dog and a cat) slept with James.

C In each blank, write the word that tells what somebody did.

1. gets _got_
2. rides _rode_
3. drinks _drank_
4. teaches _taught_
5. holds _held_

6. rides _rode_
7. teaches _taught_
8. gets _got_
9. holds _held_
10. drinks _drank_

224   *Lesson 86*

57

A Put in capitals and periods. Circle the part of each sentence that names.

(A woman) bought a new bike for her son. It had big tires. (The boy) liked the bike. (His mother) showed him how to ride the bike. He rode it to school. (His teacher) let him show the bike to the class.

B Circle the subject. Underline the part that tells more.

1. (Three older boys) went to the store.
2. (A horse and a dog) went to a stream.
3. (A man) sat on a log.
4. (They) sat on a bench.
5. (My friend and his mother) were hungry.
6. (My hands and my face) got dirty.

C

went
Mr. Smith and his son are going to the circus. They looked at lions and
made
tigers. A lion tamer had a whip in his hand. His whip is making a big noise. One
jumped   had
lion is jumping through a hoop. Mr. Smith and his son are having a good time.

Does each sentence tell what someone or something did? **X X X X**

D In each blank, write the word that tells what people did.

1. rides   _rode_
2. holds   _held_
3. teaches   _taught_
4. drinks   _drank_
5. gets   _got_
6. teaches   _taught_
7. holds   _held_
8. gets   _got_
9. rides   _rode_
10. drinks   _drank_

A Circle the subject of each sentence. Underline the part that tells more.

1. (A jet airplane) made a lot of noise.
2. (A man and his dog) went walking.
3. (He) ate lunch in the office.
4. (My brother and his friend) played in the park.
5. (A little cat) drank milk.

B Put in capitals and periods. Circle the subject of each sentence.

(Three workers) built a dog house. (A woman) nailed boards together. She used a big hammer. (A young man) put a roof on the dog house. (The workers) finished the dog house in two hours.

C In each blank, write the word that tells what somebody did.

1. drinks   _drank_
2. holds   _held_
3. rides   _rode_
4. gets   _got_
5. teaches _taught_

A Put in the missing capitals and periods.

Every student in the class read a book. Tom and Alice read a book about animals. They learned about animals that live in different parts of the world. Two students read a book about roses. That book told how to take care of roses.

B Circle the subject of each sentence. Underline the predicate.

1. (Five cats) were on the roof.
2. (They) read two funny books.
3. (A red bird) landed on a roof.
4. (A dog and a cat) played in their yard.
5. (It) stopped.

C Fill in the blanks with **He, She** or **It**.

1. My grandmother loves to walk. _She_ walks five miles every day.
2. Her brother is ten years old. _He_ is in the fifth grade.
3. Our plane will leave at four o'clock. _It_ is going to China.

58

A Put in the missing capitals and periods.

My class had a picnic. E everybody went on a bus. Our teacher brought apples and oranges. He also cooked a chicken. W we built a fire to cook the chicken.

B Change the part that names in some of the sentences to **He, She** or **It**.

(a) ~~Susan~~ loved birds. (b) *She* ~~Susan~~ wanted to build a bird house. (c) ~~Her grandfather~~ gave Susan a book about bird houses. (d) *He* ~~Her grandfather~~ told Susan to read it carefully. (e) ~~The book~~ was interesting. (f) *It* ~~The book~~ showed how to build a bird house.

C In each blank, write the word that tells what somebody did.

1. holds   held
2. gets   got
3. rides   rode
4. teaches   taught
5. drinks   drank

A Fix up the paragraph so each sentence begins with a capital and ends with a period.

A little bird fell out of a tree. Bill and his sister saw the little bird. I it was in a pile of leaves. Bill picked up the little bird. H his sister climbed up to the nest. Bill handed the bird to his sister. S she put the bird back in the nest.

B Next to each word, write the word that tells what somebody did.

1. thinks   thought
2. files   flew
3. stands   stood
4. brings   brought
5. breaks   broke
6. stands   stood
7. brings   brought
8. thinks   thought
9. breaks   broke
10. flies   flew

C Change the part that names in some of the sentences to **He, She** or **It**.

(a) The class was playing football during recess. (b) Tom had the football. (c) *He* ~~Tom~~ threw the ball as far as he could. (d) Alice jumped up and caught the ball. (e) *She* ~~Alice~~ scored a touchdown. (f) The school bell rang. (g) *It* ~~The school bell~~ told the class that recess was over.

A Circle the subject. Underline the predicate.

1. (Sara and Rodney) painted the kitchen blue.
2. (Sara) had a paintbrush.
3. (Rodney) used a roller.
4. (They) stopped to eat lunch.
5. (She) laughed.
6. (The windows) were blue.

B Next to each word, write the word that tells what somebody did.

1. stands   stood
2. thinks   thought
3. breaks   broke
4. flies   flew
5. brings   brought
6. breaks   broke
7. brings   brought
8. flies   flew
9. stands   stood
10. thinks   thought

C Fix up any sentences in the paragraph that should name **He, She** or **It**.

(a) John wanted to have a party for his birthday. (b) *He* ~~John~~ was going to be ten years old. (c) His mother planned a big party. (d) *She* ~~His mother~~ called all John's friends. (e) *She* ~~His mother~~ bought lots of party things. (f) The party started right after school. (g) *It* ~~The party~~ was a lot of fun.

A Fix up the paragraph so each sentence begins with a capital and ends with a period.

Tom threw a rock at a tree. His rock hit a beehive. the bees got very mad. they flew out of the nest. Tom ran away from the bees. many bees chased him. tom jumped into the lake. He never threw rocks at trees again.

B Circle the subject. Underline the predicate.

1. (Mr. Dunn and his son) went to the store.

2. (Mrs. Iverson) met Mrs. Lopez and her son.

3. (Two dogs) started to run around the store.

4. (Mr. Jones) was happy.

5. (They) sat in a rocking chair.

C Fix up any sentences in the paragraph that should name **He, She** or **It**.

Greg cleaned up his room last week. ~~He~~ Greg put all his toys in the closet. His grandmother was very happy. ~~His grandmother~~ She gave him a big hug.

D Next to each word, write the word that tells what somebody did.

1. flies   flew

2. brings   brought

3. breaks   broke

4. thinks   thought

5. stands   stood

E

1.   2.   3.

white	black	big	small

1. A __black__ cat sat on a __big__ chair.

2. A __white__ cat sat on a __small__ chair.

3. A __white__ cat sat on a __big__ chair.

A Fix up the paragraph so each sentence begins with a capital and ends with a period.

Snow fell all night long. Doris got up and looked outside. everything was white. Doris thought about things to do in the snow. she wanted to throw snowballs. She wanted to roll in the snow. Her mother handed her a snow shovel. Doris went out in the snow. She did not have a lot of fun.

B Fix up any sentences in the paragraph that should name **He, She** or **It**.

Sandra wanted to play baseball. ~~Sandra~~ She looked for her ball and bat. Her brother also wanted to play baseball. ~~Her brother~~ He helped her look for the ball and bat. Sandra looked in the yard. ~~Sandra~~ She found the ball and bat near the doghouse. The ball was in bad shape. ~~The ball~~ It was all chewed up.

C If a word is somebody's name, begin the word with a capital letter.

Nancy	he	truck	Tammy	James
they	Linda	Ann	Jack	my	Sam
Tina	she	window		Tim	it

D

1.   2.   3.

beach	tennis

1. __An old__ woman held a __beach__ ball.

2. __A young__ woman held a __tennis__ ball.

3. __An old__ woman held a __tennis__ ball.

E Next to each word, write the word that tells what somebody did.

1. stands   stood

2. breaks   broke

3. thinks   thought

4. brings   brought

5. flies   flew

A

  | 2. | 3.

| seat | leg | back | arm |

1. A cat sat on ___the arm of___ a chair.

2. A cat sat on ___the seat of___ a chair.

3. A cat sat on ___the back of___ a chair.

B

got
1. Tyrell ~~gets~~ a new dog.
taught
2. His sister ~~teached~~ him to ride a bike.
flew
3. The airplane ~~flied~~ over the mountain.
stood
4. Vanessa ~~standed~~ on a table.
saw
5. We ~~seen~~ an elephant at the circus.

Lesson 95—Test 9   Test Score [ ]

A   Circle the subject. Underline the predicate.

1. (A young man) walked home.

2. (It) made a big noise.

3. (My little sister) is sick.

4. (Her brother and sister) went to school.

5. (That pencil) belongs to her.

B   Fix up the paragraph so each sentence begins with a capital and ends with a period.

A   T
a̶ boy threw a rock at a tree. the rock missed the tree. The rock hit a

                              T   H
beehive. The bees got mad. they chased the boy. h̶e ran all the way home.

C   Fix up any sentences that should name **He, She** or **It.**

                        He
The cooks made pizza. ~~Tom~~ put the pizza in the oven. Tom was very

                                            She
careful. Jane took the pizza out of the oven. ~~Jane~~ told everybody that they could

                              It
eat. The pizza tasted great. ~~The pizza~~ had lots of cheese and tomatoes.

D

• An animal sat on a vehicle.   • A dog sat on a bike.   • An animal sat on a car.

1. Copy the sentence that tells about only one picture.

___A dog sat on a bike.___

2. Copy the sentence that tells about two pictures.

___An animal sat on a car.___

3. Copy the sentence that tells about all the pictures.

___An animal sat on a vehicle.___

A   Begin all parts of a person's name with a capital letter.

B J
1. b̶ill j̶ones

M W
2. m̶rs. w̶illiams

3. the doctor

4. his brother

A
5. a̶nita

S M
6. s̶am m̶iller

7. this boy

M A
8. m̶r. a̶dams

9. the girl

T
10. t̶ed

11. the nurse

M C
12. m̶rs. c̶ash

B   Fix up the paragraph so each sentence begins with a capital and ends with a period.

A   A
a̶ strong wind blew down a tree and a fence. a̶ boy and a girl saw the

                  T   T   T
broken fence. the boy got a can of paint. the girl got a hammer and nails. they

worked very hard to fix the fence.

C

brought
1. Lee ~~bringed~~ home a new dog.
thought
2. We ~~thinked~~ about it all night.
stood
3. He ~~standed~~ on the corner.
got
4. Carlos ~~gots~~ new gloves for his birthday.
taught
5. My mom ~~teached~~ me to ride a bike.

D

roof	tire	hood	trunk	headlight

1. A monkey sat on ___the hood of___ a car.

2. A monkey sat on ___the roof of___ a car.

3. A monkey sat on ___the trunk of___ a car.

E Circle the subject in each sentence. Underline the predicate.

1. (That old house) fell down.

2. (A new flower) came up in the garden.

3. (Marcus) laughed at the joke.

4. (The box) was full of money.

5. (His room) was clean.

6. (Three cows and two horses) were in the barn.

A Begin all parts of a person's name with a capital letter.

1. $\overset{M}{m}$rs. $\overset{R}{r}$obinson

2. her sister

3. $\overset{S}{s}$teve $\overset{C}{c}$rosby

4. a police officer

5. my teacher

6. tigers

7. $\overset{D}{d}$ebbie

8. $\overset{M}{m}$r. $\overset{J}{j}$ames

9. a clown

B Fill in the blanks with **He, She, It** or **They.**

1. A man and a woman ate dinner.

2. Two boys walked on the sand.

3. Our bus had a flat tire.

4. Bananas cost 68 cents.

5. The men wore red jackets.

6. That old car went fast.

1. ___They___ ate dinner.

2. ___They___ walked on the sand.

3. ___It___ had a flat tire.

4. ___They___ cost 68 cents.

5. ___They___ wore red jackets.

6. ___It___ went fast.

C Put in capitals and periods.

$\overset{A}{a}$ dog ran after a cat.$\overset{T}{t}$he animals ran through the kitchen and the living room.$\overset{T}{t}$hey ran up the stairs and down the stairs.$\overset{T}{t}$he dog ran slower and slower.$\overset{T}{t}$he cat kept going faster.$\overset{T}{t}$he dog stopped and fell over.$\overset{T}{t}$he cat was not even tired.

D Rewrite the paragraph so the underlined parts give a clear picture.

An animal fell out of a large old tree. It landed on the soft ground. A person picked it up. The person put it in a container and took it home.

A Begin all parts of a person's name with a capital letter.

1. $\overset{G}{g}$reg

2. $\overset{M}{m}$rs. $\overset{A}{a}$bbott

3. my sister

4. cowboys

5. $\overset{R}{r}$onnie $\overset{L}{l}$ee

6. a little poodle

7. $\overset{J}{j}$erry $\overset{A}{a}$dams

8. $\overset{M}{m}$r. $\overset{S}{s}$anders

9. cats

10. the fireman

11. $\overset{P}{p}$eggy

12. $\overset{M}{m}$rs. $\overset{J}{j}$ackson

B Fill in the blanks with **He, She, It** or **They.**

1. A cow and a horse drank water.

2. My shoes were wet.

3. Anna played baseball.

4. A boy shouted.

5. His sister stood in line.

6. A bottle fell off the table.

1. ___They___ drank water.

2. ___They___ were wet.

3. ___She___ played baseball.

4. ___He___ shouted.

5. ___She___ stood in line.

6. ___It___ fell off the table.

C

A woman drove an old car.$\overset{S\ had}{she\ has}$ the car for many years. She took good care of her car. She even $\overset{painted}{was\ painting}$ the car. Her car looked as good as new. $\overset{E}{e}$verybody $\overset{liked}{likes}$ that wonderful old car.

☐ **Check 1.** Does each sentence begin with a capital and end with a period?

☐ **Check 2.** Does each sentence tell what somebody or something did?

62

D Write **S** in front of each part that is a subject.
Write **P** in front of each part that is a predicate.

P 1. ran to the store
P 2. had a long tail
S 3. my dog
S 4. Troy and Chris
P 5. had four new tires

S 6. she
S 7. my sister
P 8. was on the table
S 9. two dogs and three cats
P 10. bought a yellow dress

E

1. He ~~breaked~~ *broke* his leg.
2. They ~~rided~~ *rode* a horse.
3. I ~~seen~~ *saw* my brother in the park.
4. Tamika ~~gots~~ *got* an A on the test.
5. Tyrell ~~drinked~~ *drank* a glass of water.

F Rewrite the paragraph so the underlined parts give a clear picture.

A <u>man</u> sat on <u>an object</u>. A <u>bird</u> sat on <u>him</u>. He held <u>it</u> in one hand. He tossed <u>food</u> with the other hand. Three <u>animals</u> picked up the <u>food</u>.

A Write **S** in front of each part that is a subject.
Write **P** in front of each part that is a predicate.

S 1. Jerry and Tom
P 2. walked to the store
P 3. played cards with Jill
S 4. my brother and I
S 5. three eggs

P 6. went to the movies
S 7. they
S 8. she
P 9. talked to the doctor
P 10. had fun with his friend

B

A car went past our house. It ~~has~~ *had* old tires. ~~it~~ *I* had four broken doors. The car ~~was making~~ *made* lots of noise. ~~smoke~~ *S* came out of the hood. The driver ~~is getting~~ *got* out of the car. ~~He is kicking~~ *H kicked* the car. ~~his~~ *H* car fell apart.

☐ **Check 1.** Does each sentence begin with a capital and end with a period?
☐ **Check 2.** Does each sentence tell what somebody or something did?

C Fill in the blanks with **He, She, It** or **They.**

1. Two women fixed the car.
2. My father bought a new tie.
3. The boys and girls played baseball.
4. Jill found ten dollars.
5. His bag was full of apples.
6. Those apples were not ripe.
7. Her sisters fixed Jim's car.
8. David fed the dog.

1. _They_ fixed the car.
2. _He_ bought a new tie.
3. _They_ played baseball.
4. _She_ found ten dollars.
5. _It_ was full of apples.
6. _They_ were not ripe.
7. _They_ fixed Jim's car.
8. _He_ fed the dog.

D Begin all parts of a person's name with a capital letter.

1. *A*lice
2. *M*r. *M*artinez
3. my brother
4. the doctor
5. the new boss
6. *R*obert
7. *M*rs. *A*dams
8. a big fish
9. a fire fighter
10. *S*ally
11. *C*arl *S*anders
12. that teacher

E Rewrite the paragraph so the underlined parts give a clear picture.

A <u>man</u> was carrying some food. He saw some <u>animals</u>. He dropped <u>it</u> and climbed up <u>a plant</u>. Some of the <u>animals</u> ate <u>it</u>. Some of the animals looked up at the <u>man</u>.

A

James had two good friends. Their names were *J*ill *A*dams and *R*obert *G*omez. *J*ill and *R*obert went to the same school that *J*ames went to. Their teacher was *MR*. *R*ay.

☐ **Check.** Does each part of a person's name begin with a capital? **9**

B Cross out some of the names and write **He, She, It** or **They.**

Tom and Mary went to the airport. ~~Tom and Mary~~ *They* were going to meet their dad in San Francisco. Tom had never been on a plane before. ~~Tom~~ *He* was very frightened. Tom and Mary sat together on the plane. ~~Tom and Mary~~ *They* had fun after Tom stopped worrying.

C In each blank, write the word that tells what somebody did.

1. swims _swam_
2. begins _began_
3. comes _came_
4. draws _drew_
5. takes _took_
6. draws _drew_
7. takes _took_
8. begins _began_
9. comes _came_
10. swims _swam_

63

Lesson 100

D Write **S** in front of each part that is a subject.
Write **P** in front of each part that is a predicate.

P 1. went to the circus   S 6. my sister

S 2. our family   P 7. sat under a large tree

P 3. laughed at the clowns   S 8. Tom and his sister

P 4. was very exciting   P 9. ate dinner with us

S 5. lions and tigers   S 10. they

E Rewrite the paragraph so the underlined parts give a clear picture.

She was riding a vehicle. She was in the middle of it. An animal jumped in front of it. She turned sharply. The vehicle ran into a plant. The plant damaged it.

Lesson 101

A Fix up the paragraph so that none of the sentences begin with **and** or **and then.**

Morgan threw a Frisbee to his dad. ~~And~~ It went over his dad's head. ~~And then~~ His dad ran after the Frisbee. ~~And then~~ He tripped in the mud. Morgan started to run after the Frisbee. ~~And~~ A big dog picked it up before Morgan could grab it. ~~And then~~ The dog ran away with it. ~~And then~~ Morgan chased after the dog. His dad went in the house to clean up.

B

1. draws   drew   6. begins   began

2. swims   swam   7. comes   came

3. begins   began   8. draws   drew

4. takes   took   9. swims   swam

5. comes   came   10. takes   took

C

The clowns   elephant   Sally
~~They~~ cleaned the ~~animal~~. ~~She~~ wore great big shoes and dark glasses. ~~She~~ squirted the ~~animal~~ with a hose. ~~He~~ wore a cowboy hat. ~~He~~ sat on the ~~animal~~ and scrubbed its back. ~~She~~ wore a funny suit and a tiny hat. ~~She~~ stood on a ladder. ~~She~~ poured ~~it~~ on the ~~animal~~.
(elephant, Pete, elephant, Jessica, water, elephant)

Lesson 102

A

We had a good time at the park. Tom played basketball with bob. Alice and jane went jogging. I listened to mr. anderson read from a book. my sister went swimming. we got home just in time for dinner.
(B, J, M, A, M, W)

☐ **Check 1.** Does each sentence begin with a capital and end with a period?
☐ **Check 2.** Does each part of a person's name begin with a capital letter?

B

Sandra went to the zoo yesterday. ~~And then~~ she met her friends near the monkey house. ~~And~~ the monkeys were doing tricks. Two monkeys were swinging by their tails. ~~And~~ one monkey was doing flips. ~~And then~~ Sandra and her friends went to the snack bar. ~~And~~ they bought peanuts for the monkeys.
(S, T, O, T)

C

Three horses   A jeep
~~They~~ were in a corral. ~~It~~ drove up. It started to make a loud noise. ~~They~~ were in ~~it~~. ~~He~~ grabbed a rope and jumped out of ~~it~~. ~~They~~ stayed in ~~it~~.
(Three cowboys, the jeep, the jeep, An old cowboy, Two young cowboys, the jeep)

Lesson 103

A Circle the subject. Underline the predicate.

1. (Carlos) built a fire.

2. (Susan and Vanessa) are planning a party.

3. (My old clock) was broken.

4. (It) is very cold.

5. (The horses and cows) stood in the barn.

6. (They) gave a prize to every child.

B

Everybody went to the beach. ~~And~~ Jerry and alice built a fire on the sand. ~~And then~~ Tom and bill roasted hot dogs and marshmallows. ~~And~~ Mr. jones and sammy played ball.
(A, B, J, S)

☐ **Check 1.** Did you fix each sentence that started with **and** or **and then**?
☐ **Check 2.** Does each part of a person's name begin with a capital letter?

C Write the word that tells what somebody did.

1. comes   came   4. takes   took

2. swims   swam   5. begins   began

3. draws   drew   6. thinks   thought

A

~~cooked~~
Sam and Ellen ~~are cooking~~ supper for their family. Ellen made hamburgers,
S
~~she~~ cooked them over a fire. Sam ~~makes~~ corn. ~~he was putting~~ butter and salt
made **H** *put*
on each piece. Everyone ~~likes~~ the meal.
liked

☐ **Check 1.** Does each sentence begin with a capital and end with a period?
☐ **Check 2.** Does each sentence tell what somebody or something did?

B Fix up the run-on sentences.

1. Two girls played football. ~~and~~ **T** their dad watched them. ~~and then~~ **T** they asked him if he wanted to play.

2. A boy asked his mother for some food. ~~and then~~ **S** she gave him an apple. ~~and~~ **H** he asked if he could also have some cheese. ~~and~~ **H** his mother gave him a piece of cheese.

C
Tina and Henry — grocery store — a pickup truck
They came out of the building. They walked toward it.
Tina — Henry — A girl on a bicycle
She carried it. He carried them. She waved to them.
a bottle of milk — two large bags — Tina and Henry

A Fix up the run-on sentences.

1. Mr. Clark went for a ride in the country. ~~and then~~ **H** His car ran out of gas. ~~and then~~ **H** he had to walk three miles to a gas station.

2. Kathy likes to read books. ~~and~~ **H** Her favorite book was about horses. ~~and~~ **H** her brother gave her that book.

3. Pam's mother asked Pam to mow the lawn. ~~and then~~ Pam started to cut the grass. ~~and~~ **I** it was too wet.

Lesson 105—Test 10   **Test Score** ☐

A Fix up each person's name so all parts of the name begin with a capital.

1. **N** nancy **J** jackson   6. her brother
2. **M** mrs. **W** williams   7. **M** mrs. **N** nelson
3. my father   8. an old man
4. **M** mr. **A** adams   9. **D** david **J** jordan
5. **R** robert **S** smith

B Fill in the blanks with **He, She, It** or **They.**

1. Two girls ate lunch.   1. _They_ ate lunch.
2. A cow and a horse slept in the barn. 2. _They_ slept in the barn.
3. His sister went home.   3. _She_ went home.
4. The blue pen fell off the desk.   4. _It_ fell off the desk.
5. James is sick today.   5. _He_ is sick today.
6. My friends went to a party.   6. _They_ went to a party.

C Circle the subject. Underline the predicate.

1. (My little sister) had fun at school.
2. (They) were sleeping.
3. (A man and a woman) walked in the park.
4. (Her friend) won the race.
5. (She) stopped working at noon.
6. (My green pen) cost two dollars.

A Fill in the blanks with the correct words.

Three women worked on a house.
They wore work clothes.
Milly cut a board. _She_ used a saw. _Kay_ carried three pieces of wood. _She_ carried the boards on her shoulder. _Jean_ hammered nails into the wood.

B Fix up the run-on sentences.

1. Miss Wilson saw a used bike at a store. ~~and~~ **T** the bike was red and blue. ~~and then~~ Miss Wilson bought it for her sister. (3)

2. Richard and his sister went to a movie. ~~and~~ **I** it was very funny. ~~and~~ Richard and his sister ate popcorn. ~~and then~~ **T** their mother picked them up after the movie. (4)

3. Tina built a doghouse for her dog. ~~and then~~ **S** she looked in the doghouse. ~~and~~ **F** four cats were in the doghouse with her dog. (3)

65

C

1. (Six bottles) were on the table. [V above "were"]
2. (An old lion) chased the rabbit. [V above "chased"]
3. (Jane and Sue) sat under a tree. [V above "sat"]
4. (His brother) had a candy bar. [V above "had"]

D

A woman lived near our school. Her name was mrs. jones. she was an [M J S above "mrs. jones. she"]

airplane pilot. She told us many stories about flying planes.

☐ **Check 1.** Does each sentence begin with a capital and end with a period?
☐ **Check 2.** Does each part of a person's name begin with a capital letter?

A

1. (A black pencil) fell off the table. [V above "fell"]
2. (My sister) was sick. [V above "was"]
3. (A dog and a cat) played in the park. [V above "played"]
4. (They) smiled. [V above "smiled"]
5. (Ana) sang softly. [V above "sang"]
6. (An old horse) drank from a bucket. [V above "drank"]

B

Fix up the run-on sentences in this paragraph.

Don found a lost dog. and the dog had a collar around its neck. The [T above "and the"]

collar had a phone number on it. and then Don called the phone number.

and the dog's owner answered the telephone. The owner was happy that Don [T above "and the"]

found the dog. He went to Don's house. and then Don gave the dog to the

owner.

C

For each verb that tells what somebody does, write the verb that tells what somebody did.

1. begins _began_
2. brings _brought_
3. flies _flew_
4. swims _swam_
5. takes _took_
6. comes _came_

D

Fill in the blanks with the correct words.

_____Ben_____ sat in the
wheelchair. _____He_____ wore pajamas.
The _wheelchair_ had big wheels and
little wheels. _____It_____ had a seat, a
back and two handles. _____Dora_____ held
a purse. _____She_____ wore a skirt and
a sweater. _____Ruth_____ was behind the
wheelchair. _____She_____ pushed the wheelchair.

Ruth · Ben · Dora · wheelchair

A

1. (She) jumped into the pool. [V above "jumped"]
2. (A young woman) read a book about dinosaurs. [V above "read"]
3. (My mother) had a new car. [V above "had"]
4. (They) laughed. [V above "laughed"]
5. (My brother and my sister) ate cookies and ice cream. [V above "ate"]

B

Serena went on an airplane. and she had never been on an airplane [S above "and she"]

before. She sat in a seat next to the window. and the plane took off. She fell [T above "and the"]

asleep for an hour. and she woke up. and the plane landed. Her grandmother [S above "and she", T above "and the"]

was waiting for her.

C

Fill in the blanks with the correct words.

_____James_____ and _____Alice_____
worked in the garden. _____They_____ wore
work clothes. _____Alice_____ dug a hole.
_____She_____ pushed the shovel down
with her foot. _____James_____ sawed a
branch. _____He_____ held the branch
with one hand.

James · Alice

Lesson 109

A Fix up the run-on sentences in the paragraph.

Jessica and Mark bought a pumpkin for Halloween. ~~and~~ T the pumpkin was so big that they could not carry it home. They started to roll it home. They pushed the pumpkin up a steep hill. ~~and then~~ Mark slipped. The pumpkin rolled down the hill. It smashed into a tree. ~~and~~ Jessica and Mark had lots of pumpkin pie the next day.

B

1. walked	2. smiled	3. picked	4. cried
was walking	was smiling	was picking	was crying

C Write the missing word in each item.

1. the hat that belongs to the boy — the __boy's__ hat
2. the bone that belongs to the dog — the __dog's__ bone
3. the car that belongs to her father — her __father's__ car
4. the arm that belongs to the girl — the __girl's__ arm
5. the book that belongs to my friend — my __friend's__ book
6. the toy that belongs to the cat — the __cat's__ toy

Lesson 109 **261**

Lesson 110

A Fix up the run-on sentences in the paragraph.

Ronald put his finger in a bottle. ~~and~~ H His finger got stuck in the bottle. ~~and then~~ H He asked his sister to help him. His sister got some butter. ~~and then~~ S she rubbed the butter around the top of the bottle. She pulled on the bottle. ~~and then~~ H His finger came out.

B Circle the subject. Underline the predicate. Make a **V** above every verb.

1. (The boy) walked to the store.   3. (A fish) swam in the bathtub.
   (The boy) was walking to the store.   (A fish) was swimming in the bathtub.
2. (Two girls) ate candy.
   (Two girls) were eating candy.

C

1. the dress that belongs to the girl — the __girl's__ dress
2. the tent that belongs to her friend — her __friend's__ tent
3. the toy that belongs to my cat — my __cat's__ toy
4. the watch that belongs to that boy — that __boy's__ watch
5. the hammer that belongs to his mother — his __mother's__ hammer
6. the leg that belongs to my father — my __father's__ leg

262 *Lesson 110*

Additional Practice
Test 7

A Circle the part that names. Underline the part that tells more.

1. (They) ate lunch in the park.
2. (We) saw three monkeys at the zoo.
3. (A lion and a tiger) were sleeping.
4. (An old woman) sat in front of me.
5. (My brother and my sister) were at school.
6. (Their little dog) barked all night.

B Circle the part that names. Underline the part that tells more.

1. (My shirt and my pants) were dirty.
2. (A big truck) went up the hill.
3. (She) fixed the broken window.
4. (A man and a woman) were in the car.
5. (He) walked to school.
6. (Six red ants) climbed onto the table.

Additional Practice **263**

C Fix up the sentences so they tell what people did.

1. She ~~is buying~~ bought a shirt.
2. My teacher ~~was giving~~ gave me a book.
3. The dog ~~is licking~~ licked my face.
4. Her mother ~~is finding~~ found the keys.
5. She ~~was walking~~ walked quickly.
6. They ~~are spilling~~ spilled the water.

D Fix up the sentences so they tell what people did.

1. Robin ~~is starting~~ started her car.
2. Our class ~~was having~~ had a party.
3. James ~~is digging~~ dug in the sand.
4. They ~~were pushing~~ pushed the car.
5. Mr. Adams ~~is finding~~ found his keys.
6. Alice ~~was filling~~ filled the glass.

264 *Additional Practice*

Test 8

A Put in capitals and periods.
Circle the part of each sentence that names.

(mr. James) cooked an apple pie. he put the pie on the kitchen table. a fly
flew into the kitchen. it landed on the apple pie. (mr. James) got mad. he
swung a flyswatter at the fly. he missed the fly. he hit the pie. (the pie)
splattered all over the kitchen.

B Put in capitals and periods.
Circle the part of each sentence that names.

(a little boy) threw a ball. (the ball) rolled into the street. (a big truck) ran
over the ball. (the boy) started to cry. (the truck driver) got out of the truck.
he bought a new ball for the boy.

C

Robin and her little sister ~~are going~~ *went* to the swimming pool. They
~~are wearing~~ *wore* their new bathing suits. They stayed at the pool all day. Robin
~~is sitting~~ *sat* in the sun. Her little sister ~~is playing~~ *played* in the water.

Do the sentences tell what people did? **X X X X**

D

James ~~is having~~ *had* a bad cold. He stayed home from school. He ~~is wearing~~ *wore*
pajamas all day. He ~~is sitting~~ *sat* in front of the bedroom window. His mother
~~is giving~~ *gave* him hot soup.

Do the sentences tell what people did? **X X X X**

E Fill in the blanks with **He, She** or **It**.

1. My father went swimming. _____He_____ wore his new bathing suit.
2. His bike could go very fast. _____It_____ had big tires.
3. My sister is eleven years old. _____She_____ is in fifth grade.

F Fill in the blanks with **He, She** or **It**.

1. Her brother was tired. _____He_____ did not get enough sleep.
2. My grandmother called us. _____She_____ asked us about school.
3. Her house is very big. _____It_____ has four bedrooms.

Test 9

A Circle the subject. Underline the predicate.

1. (My sister) was tired.
2. (We) tried to find it.
3. (They) flew away.
4. (That little cat) slept under the bed.
5. (My teacher and his wife) live near the school.
6. (We) saw Mr. Adams and his son.

B Circle the subject. Underline the predicate.

1. (They) sat in a big old chair.
2. (It) stopped.
3. (My red pencil) fell off the table.
4. (A cat and a dog) chased the skunk.
5. (Five striped cats) played under the house.
6. (A boy) slept on the couch.

C Fix up the paragraph so each sentence begins with a capital and ends
with a period.

A truck went up the hill. The truck went over a rock. a big barrel fell out of
the truck. the barrel rolled down the hill. it crashed into a tree. the barrel broke
into little pieces.

D Fix up the paragraph so each sentence begins with a capital and ends
with a period.

Bill's dog chased a butterfly. the butterfly flew away. the dog ran through
a big mud puddle. Bill took the dog into the bathroom. he gave the dog a bath.
the dog was not happy. She wanted to play.

E Fix up any sentences that should name **He, She** or **It**.

The children made a big sand castle at the beach. Robert made the walls.
~~Robert~~ *He* used sand that was very wet. His sister made the towers. ~~His sister~~ *She*
worked very carefully. The sand castle was three feet high. ~~The sand castle~~ *It*
looked like something you would see in a book.

F Fix up any sentences that should name **He, She** or **It**.

Linda had a birthday yesterday. ~~Linda~~ *She* was eleven years old. Her father
brought a cake to school. ~~Her father~~ *He* gave cake to each student. The cake
tasted great. ~~The cake~~ *It* had chocolate and strawberry filling.

Test 10

A Fix up each person's name so all parts of the name begin with a capital.

1. <u>A</u>lan <u>D</u>avis
2. <u>M</u>r. <u>J</u>ames
3. my teacher
4. a doctor

5. <u>R</u>obert <u>C</u>rosby
6. her sister
7. <u>D</u>avid <u>T</u>anaka
8. my best friend
9. <u>D</u>avid <u>J</u>ackson

B Fix up each person's name so all parts of the name begin with a capital.

1. <u>M</u>rs. <u>J</u>ackson
2. two cowboys
3. <u>P</u>aul <u>A</u>dams
4. <u>R</u>onnie <u>P</u>olasco
5. my sister

6. that fire fighter
7. <u>M</u>rs. <u>R</u>ay
8. <u>M</u>ichael <u>W</u>alker
9. a football player

C Fill in the blanks with **He, She** or **They.**

1. Her friends went home.
2. A dog and a cat chased the skunk.
3. Her brother came home early.
4. His toy was broken.
5. My sister drove the car.
6. The girls helped me.

1. _They_ went home.
2. _They_ chased the skunk.
3. _He_ came home early.
4. _It_ was broken.
5. _She_ drove the car.
6. _They_ helped me.

D Fill in the blanks with **He, She** or **They.**

1. That old truck went fast.
2. Apples cost 42 cents.
3. The men wore cowboy hats.
4. His mother talked on the phone.
5. Our car had a flat tire.
6. Her friends went home.

1. _It_ went fast.
2. _They_ cost 42 cents.
3. _They_ wore cowboy hats.
4. _She_ talked on the phone.
5. _It_ had a flat tire.
6. _They_ went home.

E Circle the subject. Underline the predicate.

1. (Three horses and a cow) <u>were in the barn</u>.
2. (She) <u>fell asleep</u>.
3. (A little bird) <u>flew into the house</u>.
4. (It) <u>was very large</u>.
5. (A big glass) <u>was next to the plate</u>.
6. (They) <u>stopped suddenly</u>.

F Circle the subject. Underline the predicate.

1. (His dad) <u>went into the house</u>.
2. (He) <u>talked</u>.
3. (Two girls and a boy) <u>entered the room</u>.
4. (That friendly animal) <u>smiled at us</u>.
5. (It) <u>stopped</u>.
6. (Everybody) <u>started to talk</u>.

Textbook Answer Key

Lesson 68
Part E

1. Reports.
2. No.
3. Reports.
4. No.
5. No.
6. No.

Lesson 69
Part D

1. Reports.
2. No.
3. No.
4. No.
5. Reports.
6. Reports.
7. No.

Part E

1. A tall woman held an umbrella.
2. The dog chased a cat.
3. Bill fell on the sidewalk.

Lesson 70
Part E

1. A sick man sat in a wheelchair.
2. A nurse pushed the wheelchair.
3. His sister stood next to the man.

Lesson 71
Part E

1. Mary drank a glass of water.
2. Jill sawed a board.

Part F

1. No.
2. No.
3. Reports.
4. No.
5. Reports.
6. Reports.
7. Reports.
8. No.

Lesson 72
Part D

1. Steve gave the dog a bath.
2. Martha painted part of the house.

Part E

1. Reports.
2. No.
3. No.
4. Reports.
5. No.
6. No.
7. Reports.

Lesson 73
Part E

1. Gave.
2. Dug.
3. Found.
4. Had.
5. Bought.

Part F

1. Angela rowed a boat.
2. A boy swept the floor.
3. Pam shoveled snow.

Lesson 74
Part D

1. (Idea:) Beth painted the ceiling.
2. (Idea:) Rosa read a book.

Lesson 75
Part A

1. (Idea:) A zookeeper gave a banana to a monkey.
2. (Idea:) Bob put cheese on a pizza.
3. (Idea:) A girl put a log on the campfire.

Lesson 76
Part E

1. A, B.
2. B, C.
3. B.
4. A, B, C, D.

Part F

1. (Idea:) Vic watered a plant.
2. (Idea:) A woman chopped down a tree.

Lesson 77
Part E

1. A, C.
2. B.
3. A, B, C, D.
4. B, D.

Part F

1. (Idea:) Fred and Bill watched television.
2. (Idea:) A small dog jumped through a hoop.
3. (Idea:) A young woman kicked a ball.

Lesson 78
Part D

1. Saw.
2. Went.
3. Sat.
4. Wore.
5. Ran.

Part E

1. A, D.
2. A, B, C, D.
3. C.
4. B, D.

Part F

1. (Idea:) Ramon poured soup into a pot.
2. (Idea:) Yoshi carried a log.
3. (Idea:) Jerry and Ann roasted marshmallows over a fire.

Lesson 79
Part D

1. Sat.
2. Wore.
3. Ran.
4. Saw.
5. Went.

Part E

1. A, B, C, D.
2. B, D.
3. A, B.
4. C.

Part F

1. (Idea:) That magician pulled a rabbit out of a hat.
2. (Idea:) Hiro and his sister jumped over a fence.
3. (Idea:) The new carpenter carried three boards.

Lesson 80
Part D

1. Men.
2. Children.
3. Vehicles.
4. Fire fighters.
5. Horses.

Part E

1. (Idea:) A dog and a clown walked on a tightrope.
2. (Idea:) The airplane flew under a bridge.

Lesson 81
Part E

1. Cars.
2. Boys.
3. Police officers.
4. Dogs.
5. Women.
6. Girls.

Part F

1. (Idea:) The boy kicked a football.
2. (Idea:) A girl brushed her teeth.

Lesson 82
Part E

1. B, C.
2. A.
3. A, B, C, D.
4. A, D.

Part F

1. (Idea:) That little girl sawed a branch.
2. (Idea:) A tall boy jumped into the water.

Lesson 83
Part E

1. (Idea:) A bear juggled three balls.
2. (Idea:) A monkey walked across a tightrope.

Lesson 86
Part D

1. (Idea:) The girls played basketball.
2. (Idea:) The clowns washed the elephant.

Lesson 87
Part E

1. (Idea:) The children cleaned the room.
2. (Idea:) The men crossed the stream.

Lesson 88
Part D

1. (Idea:) The girls played in the pool.
2. (Idea:) The children opened their presents.

Part F

1. A person pushed a vehicle.
2. She pushed a vehicle.
3. He pushed a vehicle.

Lesson 89
Part D

1. Melissa sat on an animal.
2. A person sat on an animal.
3. He sat on an animal.

Part F

1. (Idea:) The girls ate a meal.
2. (Idea:) The men walked through the snow.

Lesson 90
Part D (Answers will vary.)

1. Two old men went to the store.
2. My mother worked in the yard.
3. They had a good time.

Part F

1. An animal sat on a bike.
2. An animal sat on a vehicle.
3. A dog sat on a vehicle.

Lesson 91
Part E (Answers will vary.)

1. Everybody drove to town.
2. Our teacher got sunburned.
3. She paddled a canoe.

Part F

1. (Idea:) Mr. Harmon mopped the floor. He listened to the radio. (or) He wore boots.

Lesson 92
Part D

1. (Idea:) A girl caught a baseball. She stood in front of the fence. (or) She had a baseball glove.
2. (Idea:) Arthur chopped down a tree with an ax. He had big muscles. (Accept reasonable second sentence.)

Part E

1. A person pushed a car.
2. A person pushed a vehicle.
3. He pushed a truck.

Lesson 97
Part D

1. (Idea:) A huge striped snake fell out of a large old tree. The snake landed on soft ground. A young girl picked up the snake. The girl put it in a wooden basket and took it home.

Part E (Answers will vary.)

1. (Mrs. Jones) ate breakfast.
2. (Fran and Jill) ran every morning.
3. (My uncle) had new shoes.

Lesson 98
Part F

1. (Idea:) An old man with a beard sat on a large log. A parrot sat on his shoulder. He held a bag of peanuts in one hand. He threw peanuts with the other hand. Three monkeys picked up the peanuts.

Lesson 99
Part F

1. (Idea:) A large man with big muscles was carrying a cherry pie. He saw four skunks. He dropped the pie and climbed up a tree. Two little skunks ate a piece of the pie. Two big skunks looked up at him.

Part G

1. (Idea:) The window had a small crack in it.
2. (Ideas:) The house had one window on each side of the door. (or) The house had two windows.

Lesson 100
Part E

1. (Idea:) A young woman was riding a motorcycle. She was in the middle of a desert. A mountain lion jumped in front of the motorcycle. She turned sharply. The motorcycle ran into a cactus. The cactus damaged the front wheel of the motorcycle.

Part F

1. (Idea:) A boy had a big bandage on his chin.
2. (Idea:) A painter stood on top of a little ladder.

Lesson 102
Part D

1. Drew.
2. Took.
3. Came.
4. Began.
5. Swam.

Lesson 103
Part D

1. (Idea:) A striped cat sat next to the screen door.
2. (Idea:) An old man washed a long black car.

Lesson 104
Part D

1. (Idea:) A young woman sat under a small tree.

Lesson 108
Part D

1. (Idea:) The dentist sat on a stool. He gave the boy a balloon.
2. (Idea:) The man had a curly beard. He fed a baby with a spoon.

Lesson 109
Part D

1. (Idea:) The woman wore sunglasses. She drank a glass of lemonade.
2. (Idea:) The boy had a cast on his arm. He jumped over a fence.

Lesson 110
Part D

1. (Idea:) The girl wore a fancy dress. She climbed a tree.
2. (Idea:) The woman had a blindfold over her eyes. She walked across a tightrope.